A.S.A. MONOGRAPHS

General Editor: MICHAEL BANTON

4

The Social Anthropology
of Complex Societies

A.S.A. MONOGRAPHS

Published under the auspices of the Association of Social
Anthropologists of the Commonwealth

General Editor: Michael Banton

Michael Banton, editor

Edmund Leach, editor

Raymond Firth, editor

I. M. Lewis, editor

THE SOCIAL
ANTHROPOLOGY OF
COMPLEX SOCIETIES

Edited by Michael Banton

TAVISTOCK PUBLICATIONS
London · New York · Sydney · Toronto · Wellington

First published in 1966
by Tavistock Publications Limited
11 New Fetter Lane, London EC4

Second impression 1968
Third impression 1969
SBN 422 71400 3
1.3

First published as a Social Science Paperback in 1968
Second impression 1969
SBN 422 72520 X
1.2

Printed by photolithography by
Bookprint Limited, Crawley, Sussex

This volume derives from material presented at a Conference on 'New Approaches in Social Anthropology' sponsored by the Association of Social Anthropologists of the Commonwealth, held at Jesus College, Cambridge, 24-30 June 1963

Distributed in the U.S.A.
by Barnes & Noble Inc.

IN MEMORIAM

A. R. RADCLIFFE-BROWN

FIRST CHAIRMAN AND LIFE PRESIDENT
OF THE ASSOCIATION OF SOCIAL ANTHROPOLOGISTS
OF THE COMMONWEALTH

Contents

Contents

Contents

Max Gluckman and Fred Eggan

Introduction

BACKGROUND TO THE MONOGRAPHS

The several disciplines of modern anthropology – prehistoric archaeology, physical anthropology, social or sociological anthropology, cultural anthropology, and psychological anthropology – have separated out of a general anthropology which in the second half of the nineteenth century and into the twentieth century aimed to study man both as a biological and as a social being. There are still many general anthropologists, mainly in the United States but also in Europe; and the various aspects of anthropology are still taught in many universities as a combined degree. Nevertheless, by the 1930s the different disciplines were beginning to separate from one another, though some scholars were still eminent in more than one discipline. As each anthropological discipline separated out, its practitioners turned to other subjects, whose techniques and modes of analysis were more appropriate to their problems than were those of their erstwhile colleagues. Physical anthropologists depended more on the biological sciences; psychological anthropologists (who studied the interaction of culture and personality) on psychology, especially depth psychology, and psychiatry; and social anthropologists on sociology, history, political science, law, and economics. Cultural anthropologists alone continued to draw on the biological, psychological, and sociological sciences.

Outwardly the common mark of social, cultural, and psychological anthropology was that they all continued to be comparative and cross-cultural in outlook, with an emphasis on the small-scale tribal societies of the world; and for many years the study of such a society was virtually the initiation ceremony which admitted a scholar into the ranks of anthropology. Hence all anthropologists felt they had something in common, besides their joint membership in such organizations as the

American Anthropological Association and the Royal Anthropological Institute of Great Britain and Ireland.

We believe they had something more in common, drawn from their traditional unity, besides their previous, almost unique, concentration on the tribal societies. This was a continuing focusing of interest on *customs*, as having an interrelated dependence on one another, whether in forming cultural patterns, or in operating within systems of social relations, or in the structuring of various types of personality in different groups. This focus on customs in interdependence has continued to distinguish the disciplines of anthropology from the other subjects with which each branch is increasingly associated. The analysis of custom remains one of the distinctive contributions of all anthropological studies to the human sciences.

The extent to which anthropologists specialized in one or other aspect of the general subject varied in different countries. In Great Britain, the trend has steadily moved more and more to distinctive specialization as an archaeologist, a physical anthropologist, or a sociological-social anthropologist. In Oxford and Cambridge, where anthropology has been longest taught, regulations provide for general anthropological qualifications, but it is possible for students to qualify entirely in social anthropology and other social sciences, or at most to have minimal tuition in other types of anthropology. Compulsory training on the biological side is perhaps strongest for social anthropological specialists at University College, London. At other London colleges, and at the other British universities where social anthropology has been established since the last war, the subject has usually been placed in social science faculties or departments, with sociology, economics, and political science. In a few universities only are links strong with geography or psychology within a combined Honours degree.

The British Honours degree necessarily leads, except for the Cambridge Tripos system, to a reduction in the types of other subjects that can be taken by undergraduates specializing in social anthropology. This process does not operate in the American undergraduate schools of anthropology, and hence at that level students who wish to become social anthropologists take a much greater variety of subjects, and the anthropology they are taught tends to continue to cover several branches of the subject. This naturally influences graduate schools of anthropology, since their products have to be able to teach in more than one branch of anthropology, if they are appointed to small colleges (see Mandelbaum, Lasker, and Albert, 1963).

Nevertheless, in the United States most anthropologists are becoming as specialized as they are in British universities, and are correspondingly associating with various cognate disciplines according to their type of specialization. Owing to the greater size of the country, and the far greater number of universities and of anthropologists, there is in the United States a greater variety of types of anthropologist than in the British Commonwealth. It is in the States that cultural and psychological anthropology flourish in addition to the social anthropology, physical anthropology, linguistics, and prehistoric archaeology that are represented in Britain. The flourishing of these several branches of anthropology in the States is probably fertilized, too, by the absence of the Honours degree system: there is a more varied interdisciplinary contact, which continues beyond the undergraduate level.

The increasing specialization of British social anthropologists with a decreasing interest on their part in prehistoric archaeology, physical anthropology, and cultural anthropology, in 1946 led the practitioners of the subject in Britain – then under a score – to form the Association of Social Anthropologists of the Commonwealth. Though they wished still to support the Royal Anthropological Institute, they considered that they had specific and limited interests, sufficiently distinct from those of general anthropology, to require the support of a specific organization. This has meant, for example, that social anthropologists in Britain have had an organized means of giving evidence on their own problems to commissions advising the British Government on higher education and research, besides evidence given by the Royal Anthropological Institute for anthropology in general. The process of *partial* separation from general anthropology continued until, in 1960, the social anthropologists joined with sociologists and social psychologists to form a new Sociology Section of the British Association for the Advancement of Science. Two of the five presidents of the Section to date have been social anthropologists. Social anthropologists still participate in the older Anthropology and Archaeology Section, but they submit more papers to, and attend in greater numbers at, meetings of the new section.

Between 1946 and 1962 the Association of Social Anthropologists of the Commonwealth increased its membership from under a score to over one hundred and fifty, even though election to membership required normally both the holding of a teaching or research post in the Commonwealth and the attainment of either a post-graduate degree (usually a doctorate) or substantial publication. Meetings of the Association in Britain ceased to be small gatherings of perhaps a dozen people, and were attended by between thirty and sixty members.

In 1962 Professor Raymond Firth, then Chairman of the Association, proposed that it should try to raise the funds to invite a dozen American social anthropologists to one of its meetings. He suggested that since the milieux in which American social anthropologists worked were so much more varied than the milieu of British social anthropologists, it would be profitable to see what was common between us and where we differed, in a series of papers on 'New Approaches in Social Anthropology'. He pointed out that though there were many individual contacts between some members of the Association and American colleagues, many British and Americans had not met one another: moreover, we had never had a joint, organized stocktaking. He further suggested that papers should be read only by scholars who had entered the subject since the war: so the phrase 'new approaches' signifies that the papers collected in these four volumes present the problems and views of a younger generation of anthropologists.

When the Association enthusiastically adopted Firth's proposal, there was no corresponding organization of social anthropologists in the U.S.A. with whom there could be discussions and arrangements. The Association therefore more or less thrust on Professor Fred Eggan of the University of Chicago the task of representing American social anthropologists. It did so for several reasons, besides his own standing as a social anthropologist. The late Professor A. R. Radcliffe-Brown, who had been for the first years of the Association's

existence its Life President, and to whose memory this series
of A.S.A. Monographs is dedicated, had taught at Chicago
from 1931 to 1937. Eggan had succeeded, so to speak, to Radcliffe-Brown's position, and under the Roman rule of universal
succession might be regarded as representing him. Above all,
under Radcliffe-Brown's influence there had developed in
Chicago perhaps the strongest single group of *social* anthropologists in the U.S.A. Eggan agreed to help organize the meeting,
but insisted, of course, that his British colleagues should select
the dozen American scholars whom they wished to hear. With
great difficulty, the British, eventually by vote, chose a dozen
from the large number they would have liked to invite. If there
seems a bias to Chicago, or Chicago-trained Americans (as one
or two of the others rather ironically suggested), the British
are responsible, and not Eggan. The American Anthropological
Association agreed to sponsor a request for support, and the
National Science Foundation generously financed the Americans'
journey to Britain.

The programme, to which twice as many British as Americans
contributed papers, was divided into four main sections. Two
to three papers were presented in a group, and discussion was
then opened by either an American or a British anthropologist
– again, those opening the discussions were selected from the
post-war generation, though more senior anthropologists were
allowed to join in the general discussion. But these Monographs
are not a report on the proceedings of the Conference. They
embody theoretical papers by twenty younger anthropologists,
who have amended their arguments, where they felt it necessary,
after listening to the comments of their colleagues. Effectively
the papers present, therefore, growing-points in social anthropology as seen by a new generation of practitioners.

Two years passed between the time when Firth, as Chairman
of the Association, made his original proposal, and the meeting
itself, which was held in Jesus College, Cambridge, in June
1963. By that time Gluckman had succeeded Firth as Chairman,
and on him, and the yet-again conscribed Eggan, has fallen the
task of introducing the Monographs. It has been a difficult
task: the papers cover a range of ethnographic areas and of
problems which they cannot themselves compass competently.

Hence this Introduction makes no attempt to assess the substantive problems and solutions suggested in the papers. Instead, it tries to pull together the kinds of issue which crop up as interesting the contributors in several of the papers.

There was also a major technical difficulty. The papers are published in four separate volumes, covering, respectively:

1. The relevance of models for social anthropology;
2. Political systems and the distribution of power;
3. Anthropological approaches to the study of religion;
4. The social anthropology of complex societies.

Since the Introduction was planned to cut across all four volumes, we decided to write a single text and print it in each volume. Various readers may approach the series through any of the four. The arabic figures 1, 2, 3, and 4 indicate in which of the monographs is located an essay referred to in the Introduction.

SPECIALIZATION AND SPREAD: LINKS WITH THE SOCIAL SCIENCES

The specialization of social anthropologists in a separate discipline, and the extent to which they have turned to sociology and political science, are particularly marked in these monographs. This is not surprising in the volumes on political problems (2) and on complex societies, including both peasantries and urban areas (4), where the problems dealt with are common to the three disciplines. As it happens, the other disciplines that are commonly grouped in the social sciences – economics and law – are not cited.

This is partly a matter of chance. We could provide for only a limited number of papers, and arrangements had been made to have a paper on the use of economic models in social anthropology by Mrs Lorraine Baric; but at the crucial time she went to Yugoslavia to do field-research.

Two papers do deal with 'economic problems', in the widest but not the technical sense of 'economics'. The first is by Marshall Sahlins, 'On The Sociology of Primitive Exchange', in Monograph 1. Though by its title this might be thought to deal with economic problems, its actual emphasis is on 'sociology'. It considers types of exchange in terms of degrees of reciprocity as these alter along a scale of contexts of tribal social relations, from the most personal to the least personal – if we reduce a complex analysis to a single sentence. Sahlins makes no reference to economic theorizing as such, and indeed part of the discussion of his paper turned on this point.

Eric Wolf carries out a somewhat similar analysis of morphological changes in 'Kinship, Friendship, and Patron-Client Relations in Complex Societies' (4). In this essay, Wolf examines the kinds of situation in terms of ecological and economic situations in which kinship, friendship, and patron-client relationships respectively are dominant outside the nuclear family. No more than with Sahlins, would one expect this problem to lead Wolf into the use of economic theory as such. Save for one citation from Schumpeter, he does not rely on the economists.

The absence of reference to economic theory in the papers hence means that one approach, whether it be new or old, is not covered in these four monographs. We think it is true to say that technical economics has had less influence on social anthropological research than other social sciences have had, possibly because of its highly abstract nature. In the Register of the Association of Social Anthropologists less than 3 in a 100 members list 'economics' among their special interests, and there are also few specialists in the U.S.A. Yet before the war, among other senior anthropologists, Firth, originally trained as an economist, had used the technical concepts of economics to good effect for a tribal society in his *Primitive Polynesian Economy* (1939) and, after the War, for a peasant society in his *Malay Fishermen* (1946). More recently, a number of younger anthropologists, some with training in economics, have used this training impressively. But this is perhaps more marked among those who have studied peasant societies, than among those who have studied tribes, as is shown, perhaps, in *Capital, Saving and Credit in Peasant Societies* (Firth & Yamey (eds.), 1964), a symposium containing essays by nine younger British social anthropologists, by four Americans, and by one Norwegian who was trained partly in Britain.

The Association of Social Anthropologists hopes in the near future to publish a monograph in which the use of theoretical economics in recent work by British scholars will be considered.

When these symposia were planned, arrangements had also been made to have at least one paper on problems in the field of law. Illness prevented P. J. Bohannan from preparing this. The absence of any treatment of tribal law, and more generally of processes of social control, does not reflect the extent to which these problems have interested social anthropologists in recent decades, particularly since the publication of Llewellyn and Hoebel's *The Cheyenne Way: Conflict and Case Law in Primitive Jurisprudence* (1941). That book, and Hoebel's earlier work, inspired a number of studies on jurisprudential problems, particularly on juristic method in the judicial or arbitral process, among both American and British social anthropologists. This work has drawn largely, if sometimes indirectly, on American sociological jurisprudence. This field of research is therefore not covered in the Monographs.

Here, then, are two social sciences not drawn on for this symposium.

References outside those to the work of social anthropologists are clearly most numerous to sociologists – for example, to sociometric work and to the work of the sociologists Ginsberg, Homans and W. F. Whyte, by Adrian Mayer in his treatment of 'The Significance of Quasi-Groups in the Study of Complex Societies' (4). J. Clyde Mitchell in the same volume discusses 'Theoretical Orientations in African Urban Studies' and he begins by stating that 'differences in behaviour as between people in the town and in the country have for long been the topic of study of sociologists and other social scientists in Europe and America . . .'. Though Mitchell cites only a few of these sociologists, their work clearly has influenced not only Mitchell, but also the numerous other anthropologists who have studied urban areas in Africa and who are cited by Mitchell.

But it would seem that, leaving aside Durkheim, whose school's influence on social anthropology has always been marked, the influence of Weber on younger social anthropologists in recent years has been considerable. If anything, that influence is under-represented in these essays: it has been very marked in a number of monographs, as in L. A. Fallers's *Bantu Bureaucracy* (no date: about 1956). With the influence of Weber – and partly inspired by his writings – goes the influence of Talcott Parsons among modern sociologists.

Perhaps the most cited and influential of modern sociologists in these monographs is R. K. Merton. His discussions of levels of theory, and of the distinction between manifest and latent functions, have always been exploited by anthropologists; and Melford Spiro uses them in his essay on religion in Monograph 3. But generally it is the increasing interest in the more meticulous analysis of social roles (referred to below) which inspired the writers to draw on Merton's treatment of role-sets – Ward Goodenough in 'Rethinking "Status" and "Role" ' (1), Aidan Southall on roles in different political systems (2), and Ronald Frankenberg in an essay on the changing structure of roles in different types of British communities (3), use Merton, appreciatively and critically.

Parsons too has influenced anthropologists' thinking about this key concept. There are also indications of a growing importance here of the work of Erving Goffman – himself influenced by the work of social anthropologists – on how people operate their roles. Goodenough has drawn markedly on Goffman's books on *The Presentation of Self in Everyday Life* (1959) and *Encounters* (1961). Frankenberg argues that there is a convergence between the ideas of Goffman and those developed in British social anthropology, especially by Barnes, Gluckman, and Turner.

These references must be sufficient to show how much social anthropologists are now drawing on the cognate subject of sociology. The essays thus reflect, in research and analysis, the tendency in both countries for social anthropology and sociology to be taught either in one department or in closely linked departments.

The references above are to certain types of sociology. No essay makes use of demographic analysis – but Mitchell's and a couple of other essays refer to the importance of demographic analysis, which in general has been inadequately used by social anthropologists in their reports on communities. However, it is worth noting here that anthropologists such as Mitchell and

J. A. Barnes have, in their treatment of suitable problems, been contributing to theory in demographic studies.

In their Introduction to *African Political Systems* (1940), Fortes and Evans-Pritchard wrote that: 'We have not found that the theories of political *philosophers* [italics added] have helped us to understand the societies we have studied and we consider them of little scientific value . . .' (at p. 5). At least one reviewer asked why they did not draw on the work of political *scientists*. Since Fortes and Evans-Pritchard, with *African Political Systems*, virtually established 'political anthropology', their successors have turned increasingly to political scientists for assistance in their analysis. We have already cited Fallers's use of Weber's hypotheses in his study of Soga bureaucracy, and many other monographs on political problems have used Weberian ideas as well as works by those who are more specifically political scientists or constitutional historians. Every essay in Monograph 2 refers to works in political science. The most-cited work is Easton's study of *The Political System* (1953), and his article on 'Political Anthropology' in *Biennial Review of Anthropology* (1959). Easton, in Lloyd's words (4), 'took time from his studies of modern societies to examine the progress made by social anthropologists. [Easton] castigates the failure of the anthropologists to develop any broad theoretical orientation to politics, ascribing this to their preoccupation with general problems of social control, conflict, and integration and their reluctance to define the respective limits of political and other – social, religious, economic – systems. Easton offers a classification of African political systems which is based upon the differentiation in political roles. . . .'

We are tempted to point out that in the kinds of societies traditionally studied by social anthropologists political, economic, religious, and social systems are in fact often not differentiated, and to reply that political scientists have not themselves made so clear a definition of political systems. But, reviewing the essays under consideration, Easton's own suggestion about the classification of political systems in terms of differentiation in roles fits in with a main concern of recent anthropology – marked in Aidan Southall's essay on 'A Critique of the Typology of States and Political Systems' (2).

Introduction

For the rest, the social anthropologist in his analysis of political problems seems to turn to whatever source, outside of anthropology, he feels can assist his specific analysis. Thus when F. G. Bailey consider 'Decisions by Consensus in Councils and Committees: with special reference to village and local government in India' (2), he uses work by Morris-Jones, a political scientist, on India; Wheare's now classic survey of *Government by Committee* (1955); a study of contemporary parties and politics in Japan; and F. M. Cornford's witty analysis of Cambridge University politics, *Microcosmographia Academica* (1908). Nicholas, in a comparative analysis of 'Factions' (2), equally uses a small number of political science studies. We are not suggesting that these writers use all – or even the most important – relevant sources from political science: indeed, we ourselves know of others they might have used. We indicate here only that there is a readiness to turn to political science, and Bailey's essay has more references to works by political scientists than to works by other anthropologists. Political anthropology, at least, is linking up with its cognate discipline: and this clearly is not difficult, since the concepts and analytic framework of political science are not too diverse from those of social anthropology. No new techniques have to be learned to master them.

SPECIALIZATION AND SPREAD: LINKS WITH BIOLOGY, PSYCHOLOGY, AND CULTURAL ANTHROPOLOGY

In contrast to this turn towards sociology of various kinds and to at least some fields of political science, plus the under-represented use of economics and law, we note relatively few references to cultural anthropology, psychological anthropology, psychology, and the biological sciences. In the volume on religion (3) there are references to the work of Margaret Mead, partly in the particular ethnographic context of Bali in which she worked with Gregory Bateson. This is in Clifford Geertz's essay on 'Religion as a Cultural System'. He begins by stating that the detailed studies of religion in particular societies which have characterized social anthropology are in 'a state of general stagnation', suffering under what 'Janowitz has called the dead hand of competence'. Geertz summarizes the achievements of anthropological study of religion as: 'Yet one more meticulous case-in-point for such well-established propositions as that ancestor worship supports the jural authority of elders, that initiation rites are means for the establishment of sexual identity and adult status, that ritual groupings reflect political oppositions, or that myths provide charters for social institutions and rationalizations of social privilege may well finally convince a great many people, both inside the profession and out, that anthropologists are, like theologians, firmly dedicated to proving the indubitable.'

We do not believe that these summary statements at the opening of Geertz's essay are quite fair assessments of the acute and complicated analyses actually made by social anthropologists of ancestor cults, initiation ceremonies, political rituals, and the social context of myths, exemplified in the three essays on religion in specific societies in the same volume – by V. W. Turner on 'Colour Classification in Ndembu Ritual', by R. Bradbury on 'Fathers, Elders, and Ghosts in Ẹdo Religion', and by E. Winter on 'Territorial Groupings and Religion among the Iraqw'. Geertz has himself written a notable analysis (1960) of a single society's religions.

Geertz is clearly being critical of his own, as well as of his colleagues', work, in order to plead for a much wider treatment of the general 'cultural dimension of religious analysis'. And he is not unique among younger anthropologists in feeling that the social anthropological analysis of religion by itself is inadequate. We take it that this mode of analysis is restricted to examining the role of religion, with emphasis on custom, rite, and belief, in social relations; and we believe that those who follow this procedure realize that they are not explaining 'the whole of religion'. They accept that they are analysing religion in only one of its dimensions, and that other dimensions have to be analysed by other types of discipline, using different techniques and perhaps examining other types of data. Clearly any set of phenomena as complicated as religion – indeed any social complex – for total understanding has to be subjected to investigation by several disciplines.

Introduction

We believe that most social anthropologists would accept this. Melford Spiro in his essay on 'Religion: Problems of Definition and Explanation' (3) states in his 'Conclusion' to his argument 'that an adequate explanation for the persistence of religion requires both psychological (in this instance, psycho-
- analytical) and sociological variables'. Religion, or family structure, or motivations, can be taken variously as independent or dependent variables. Spiro continues: 'But many studies of religion, however, are concerned not with the explanation of religion, but with the role of religion in the explanation of society. Here, the explanatory task is to discover the contributions which religion, taken as the independent variable, makes to societal integration, by its satisfaction of sociological wants. This is an important task, central to the main concern of anthropology, as the science of social systems. We seriously err, however, in mistaking an explanation of society for an explanation of religion which, in effect, means confusing the sociological functions of religion with the bases for its performance.' In his introductory paragraphs to his essay on Iraqw ritual (3) Winter makes the same clarification.

We have cited Spiro at length because it is in the study of religion that some social anthropologists have manifested a reluctance to accept that a specifically social anthropological analysis, giving an admittedly limited explanation, provides anything like an adequate explanation. The essays by Geertz and Spiro exhibit some of this feeling, which has appeared also in work published elsewhere, by Britons as well as Americans. Where they invoke psychology, not all of them follow Spiro in calling for some form of depth-psychology. The psychic framework employed may be an intellectualist one, in which the explanatory value for the observers is emphasized, as in the claim that the difference between tribal and universalistic rituals stems from the way people in tribal societies construct their model of the universe on the model they abstract from their own social relations (Horton, 1964).

Spiro and Winter clarify the issues involved. To understand religion, in a commonsense use of 'understand', [at least] both sociological and psychological explanations are required. The sociological – that is, the social anthropological – analysis alone is an explanation of the role of religion in social relations; and a psychological analysis alone is an explanation of the role of religion in the functioning of the personality. Nevertheless, we note that there is this dissatisfaction with the limited extent of social anthropological analysis in this field, which does not show in the treatment of political and a number of other problems.

Spiro's remains a general, abstract essay. Geertz's interestingly enough after his castigatory opening, is largely taken up with a penetrating analysis of a specific situation in Java. With all respect, we believe that there is not 'a state of general stagnation' in the subject: the evidence of several monographs shows that social anthropological understanding of religion and ritual in specific societies continues to advance. Geertz calls for a study of symbols: we consider this is illuminatingly achieved in Turner's essay on colour symbolism among the Ndembu. Geertz 'slights' such well-established propositions as that 'ancestor worship supports the jural authority of elders': we consider that Bradbury's essay on the role of ghosts and spirits among the Edo, in a comparative background, and Winter's similar attempt to illuminate the specific variants of spirit-cult organization among the Iraqw, show by contrast how steady, deep, and wide is the penetration of the subject's understanding here.

Moreover, a discipline may advance by the working out logically of basic theoretical propositions, some of which are perhaps based on observation. This applies to theoretical economics and to some aspects of Parsons's theory of action in sociology. Social anthropology has not shown a corresponding development, save perhaps in some of Lévi-Strauss's analyses. Advance may also be achieved by the formulation of a series of propositions, based on observation. In the natural sciences, a number of these propositions have been cumulatively brought under a hierarchy of increasingly embracing laws. Social anthropology, like sociology and political science, has numerous propositions at the first level. It may lack widely embracing laws to cover many of these, but, like sociology and political science, it does have some theories of the middle range, as Merton (1958), with others, has phrased the situation. These middle-range theories are applied within a 'general orientation towards substantive materials' (ibid, pp. 87-88).

The kind of general approach to their data which social anthropologists have developed is illustrated throughout these essays: an insistence by most that there are interdependencies between both social relations and customs, and further associations between these interdependencies. Analysis of these interdependencies is often set in an evolutionary framework, even if it be a morphological rather than a temporal one, as the essays by Sahlins on primitive exchange (1), Wolf on kinship, friendship, and patron-client relations (4), and Mitchell and Frankenberg on the rural to non-rural continuum (4) well illustrate. The same framework is used by Lloyd and Southall, to some extent, in their essays on the typology of political systems (2). Yet social anthropology, judging by these essays, still lacks the kind of fundamental orientation found, for example, in Marxist sociology.

Individual propositions, stated baldly out of the context of this orientation, and of both field situation and corpus of allied propositions, may appear to be truistic – and hence banal. But the skill of anthropologists, like that of practitioners of the cognate disciplines, lies to a large extent still in their ability to apply, and weigh the application of, selected propositions to specific situations. This may be done within a single situation, with comparative checking implicit, or it may be done with occasional explicit comparison, or it may be done outright as a comparative study. On the whole, these procedures, and attempts to develop them with refinement of the basic propositions, appear to us to dominate these essays on 'new approaches' in the subject. The striving is after clarification; elimination of muddles; clearing away of concepts that, though once useful, now appear to be too gross and to block analysis; and the formulation of better theories of the middle range. These tendencies are marked in the essays by Geertz and Spiro, though these are also the only essays which press for, and aim at, much higher-level theories.

One attempt to formulate further theories of the middle range is appropriately referred to in this section on links with psychology and cultural anthropology. Wolf's analysis of the

contexts in which kinship, friendship, and patron-client relations are respectively dominant in complex societies (4), is in
some respects complementary to Sahlin's essay on the changing
contexts of exchange in tribal societies (1): basically, it is *social*
anthropological in tackling its problems, with the emphasis on
making a living, handling relations with authorities, etc. But
at the end of the essay, Wolf suggests that the varying texture
of relations with kin, friends, and patrons or clients may have
'a point of encounter with what has sometimes been called the
national character approach'. Examining works in this field,
he is struck by the fact that 'they have utilized – in the main –
data on the interpersonal sets discussed in [his] paper, and on
the etiquettes and social idioms governing them'. Wolf cites
three instances, and concludes: 'It is obvious that such descriptions and analyses do not cope with the institutional features of
national structure. Yet it is equally possible that complex
societies in the modern world differ less in the formal organization of their economic or legal or political systems than in the
character of their supplementary inter-personal sets. Using
the strategy of social anthropology, moreover, we would say
that information about these sets is less meaningful when
organized in terms of a construct of homogeneous national
character, than when referred to the particular body of social
relations and its function, partial or general, within the supplementary or parallel structure underlying the formal institutional framework. . . . The integration of the great society
requires the knitting of these interstitial relations.'

We have cited Wolf at length because he appears to us
explicitly to map in outline common ground between several
of the essays which deal with what can be the social anthropological contribution to the study of complex societies. It is
clearly accepted that a study of large-scale institutional frame-
works such as the economic, or the administrative and political,
falls to the lot of economists, political scientists, and sociologists. With this acceptance, goes the assumption, to quote
Wolf again, of a possibility 'that complex societies of the modern
world differ less in the formal organization of their economic or
legal or political system than in the character of their supplementary interpersonal sets'. Anthropologists of all kinds have

always been fascinated by the variety of human behaviour, even when they have sought uniformity and generality in that variety. So that aside from their interest in the small-scale, which fits with their techniques of observation, they tend to concentrate on those features of complex — as of tribal — societies where there are some distinctive sets of customs which require to be explained. We think this tendency shows in Bailey's treatment of committees and Nicholas's of factions in modern India (2).

This tendency is particularly marked in Monograph 4 specifically devoted to complex societies. In his essay on 'Theoretical Orientations in African Urban Studies' Mitchell begins by stating that 'in Africa, as elsewhere, urban studies raise the same questions'. He continues by stating that 'the focus of sociological interest in African urban studies must be on the way in which the behaviour of town-dwellers fits into, and is adjusted to, the social matrix created by the commercial, industrial, and administrative framework of a modern metro-polis – having regard to the fact that most African town-dwellers have been born and brought up in the rural hinterland of the city, in which the cultural background is markedly dissimilar from that of the city'. After discussing social surveys and inten-sive studies, he distinguishes between 'historical' or 'processive' change to cover overall changes in the social system, and 'situational change', which covers changes in behaviour 'fol-lowing participation in different social systems'. In dealing with both these types of change, Mitchell emphasizes the importance of relations of kinship and friendship – thus he faces the same problems as Wolf. He is then concerned to distinguish structural from categorical relationships, before passing to emphasize the importance of studying 'the network of personal links which individuals have built around themselves in towns'. Seeing problems very similar to those seen by Wolf, he suggests that the study of networks may show 'the way in which norms and values are diffused in a community, and how the process of "feedback" takes place.' In these studies, gossip, joking relations, historical antecedents, can all be taken into account.

In Monograph 4 Adrian Mayer treats, with technical detail, a similar set of problems, in an essay on 'The Significance of

Quasi-Groups in the Study of Complex Societies'. He too emphasizes the importance of networks and action-sets of relations, as against groups, and tries to clarify and refine those concepts. He applies them to an Indian electoral struggle. He concludes: 'It may well be that, as social anthropologists become more interested in complex societies and as the simpler societies themselves become more complex, an increasing amount of work will be based on ego-centred entities such as action-sets and quasi-groups, rather than on groups and sub-groups' – the latter being, presumably, what Wolf calls 'the formal organization' of complex societies.

Burton Benedict, in the same monograph, considers 'Sociological Characteristics of Small Territories' such as Mauritius. He sets his task as an assessment of the relation between the scale of society and: the number, kinds, and duration of social roles; types of values and alternatives; magico-religious practices; jural relations; political structure; and economic development. The first three are traditionally in the field of social anthropology. What is more significant is that in handling the last two sets of problems, Benedict emphasizes that the elites involved are small, and, though not explicitly, we are back with the problems of quasi-groups, networks, and action sets.

Frankenberg's discussion (also in 4) of changes in the structure of social roles and role-sets in a range of British 'communities', from the truly rural to the housing-estate, hinges again on changes, in both groups and quasi-groups, which determine the structure of individuals' varied roles; but he illustrates too the urgent need to study custom, belief, and ceremonial as our specific contribution.

We see here, then, a common orientation, and a drive towards a common set of concepts, as social anthropologists tackle the problems of urban societies and of changing tribal and peasant communities. Some of them argue explicitly that these concepts developed to handle 'complex' situations, would also illuminate studies of tribal societies. These studies deal with problems which social anthropologists share with sociologists and political scientists, rather than with other types of anthropologists, and it may be that the *social* part of the title 'social anthropology' will begin to outweigh the *anthropology*. Yet there remain speci-

Introduction

fic interests derived from the common tradition of *anthropology*.

Only in the study of religion do any of the contributors argue for the essential place of some psychological treatment. As it happens, the studies of kinship relations included occur only in the volume on 'the relevance of models': the whole fruitful field of study in psychological anthropology, represented by Lewinson, Linton, Mead, Whiting, and many others, is not referred to. This may be partly a reflection of who was asked to contribute, and what those invited decided to write on. Yet these essays show that there is a whole dimension of marital and parental relations which, it is accepted, can be studied without reference to psychological concomitants.

Strikingly, the feeling that it is justifiable for social anthropologists to work without reference to studies in psychology, is shown in Joe Loudon's essay on 'Religious Order and Mental Disorder' in a South Wales community (4). Loudon is a qualified medical, who later turned to anthropology. He has been trained in psychiatry, and has worked for the British Medical Research Council on the position of the mentally ill in a community, and the community's reaction to such people. His research is into attitudes, yet he works with the same basic concepts as his colleagues: he analyses social roles in terms of class and social status, religious affiliation, length of residence in the district, etc., in relation to conscious attitudes, involving the allocation of culpability, assumption that mental disorder is illness, and so forth. So too in studying the religious order he is concerned with statements about the role of crises in personal relations, in so far as these affect reactions to mental disorder. He looks also at patterns of social mobility, and at the effect of these on individuals' social networks. His general mode of analysis 'fits' with the analyses we have just discussed: significantly, to handle social attitudes, he does not turn to work in social psychology.

GENERAL ORIENTATIONS

In this background of realignment with cognate disciplines, the essays show two main trends. The first is an insistence that certain concepts that were acceptable in preceding decades are now too gross to be useful, and have to be refined, or that they may even block further analysis. The second is the feeling that more work should be done to pull together, in a comparative framework, observations that are discrete in terms of subject-matter or of ethnographic milieu. Obviously, these are the two possibilities that offer themselves, aside from carrying out studies that repeat what has been done before – and we do not regard such studies as useless. One can either penetrate more deeply into an area of problems, or pull together what has already been done.

There are many new ideas in these essays, but no author has tried to put forward an altogether new theoretical approach – or even to recast the basic orientations of the subject. In making the statement, we do so with full allowance for Spiro's insistence (3) that to study religion, as against studying society, a psychological approach is as essential as a social anthropological one. Geertz pleads (3) for a new look – via philosophy, history, law, literature, or the 'harder' sciences – at religion, but he nevertheless considers that 'the way to do this is not abandon the established traditions of social anthropology in this field, but to widen them'. He still looks to Durkheim, Weber, Freud, and Malinowski as 'inevitable starting-points for any useful anthropological theory of religion'. The specific problems he deals with – suffering, evil, chance, the bizarre, ethics – are not in themselves new fields of problems, though his proferred solutions to the problems may be new.

The basic orientation in these essays is therefore still the acceptance that the events which comprise human behaviour exhibit regularities whose forms are mutually interdependent, over and above their interdependence, in the personality-behaviour systems of each individual actor. As Radcliffe-Brown put it, there are social systems whose structures can be analysed. An interdependence of cultural institutions, each of which has an elaborate structure, would perhaps be the parallel Malinowskian formulation. Given this general orientation, it seems to us that these social anthropologists have a much looser idea of a social system, or of a complex of institutions, than Radcliffe-Brown or Malinowski had. A social system is not seen in analogy with an organic system, whose structure is maintained by some customary procedure, as it was by Radcliffe-

Brown. Nor is there acceptance of Malinowski's ideas of the function of institutions in relation to a hierarchy of needs: Spiro (3) specifically criticizes this approach.

These 'tight' models of social systems or cultures were abandoned by the inter-war generation of social anthropologists (see Redfield, 1955). But those anthropologists continued to worry about the nature of social systems and cultures, or the structure of social fields. On the evidence of these essays, the younger anthropologists no longer consider this worry justified: at least none of them has dealt with that kind of problem at length, or as basic to his analysis. Geertz (3) goes to some pains to discuss 'culture'. Spiro (3) has some discussion of what a system is. David Schneider, in an essay on 'Some Muddles in the Models: or, How the System Really Works' (1) considers the competing, and hotly argued, opposed views of two sets of anthropologists on descent and affinity: and he states that one cause of their disputation is that they need to be clearer about whether the theory is advanced to cover the structure of a social system, or whether it is about how the individual finds his way in that system. He feels that the argument will get nowhere, unless this point is clarified. That is, he asks for clarity on problems set, and he is not concerned with the epistemology of the subject. We hope that our younger colleagues feel that earlier disputation on the nature of social systems and social fields, or on the nature of culture, clarified the issues, if only through the substantive work done; and that the disputation was not always meaningless.

When we say there seems to be no new general orientation shown, but a determination to get on with the job with established orientations, we must mention the 'new' evolutionary school of Leslie White, represented here by Sahlins's essay on primitive exchange in Monograph 1. The evolutionary argument is not marked in this particular essay, and on the whole Sahlins's analysis is similar in structure to the arguments of Wolf about kinship, friendship, and patron-client relations (4), of Frankenberg about the association of role types with forms of British community (4), of Benedict about the characteristics of small-scale territories (4), and of Lloyd and Southall about the typology of African political systems (2). The type of argument is shown in the cautious hypothesis about primitive money which, among others, is advanced, by Sahlins: 'it [primitive money] occurs in conjunction with unusual incidence of balanced reciprocity in peripheral social sectors. Presumably it facilitates the heavy balanced traffic'. This is precisely the sort of hypothesis about an association between social variables which is commonly sought by anthropologists, and is well illustrated in the four other essays just cited. But Sahlins continues: 'The conditions that encourage primitive money are most likely to occur in the range of primitive societies called tribal and are unlikely to be served by band or chiefdom development ... Not all tribes provide circumstances for monetary development and certainly not all enjoy primitive money, as that term is here understood. For the potentiality of peripheral exchange is maximized only by some tribes. Others remain relatively inner-directed.'

We consider that, despite the turning against the simple evolutionary theories of the nineteenth century, some kind of evolutionary, or morphological, framework has been implicit in most comparative work in social anthropology. We say, 'or morphological', because many scholars have avoided an outright evolutionary statement in order to evade temporal implications. Radcliffe-Brown did this, but he believed strongly in social evolution. The result is that, aside from their important theses on the relation between use of energy and social forms, the new evolutionists, as Sahlins's essay shows, are trying to handle associations of concomitant variations, rather than items of culture, in somewhat similar ways to their colleagues. Nevertheless, we note that this new evolutionary theorizing is here represented only in the interstices, rather than in the central part, of Sahlins's essay.

REFINEMENT OF CONCEPTS

We have said that one main line of approach in these monographs, represented in several essays, is the refinement of standard concepts, in hopes of penetrating more deeply into the structure of social life. This tendency is marked in the several discussions of social roles. Even before Linton in 1936 advanced his definitions of 'status' and 'role', the handling of these phenomena was important in social anthropology: one has only to think of Radcliffe-Brown's concern with social personality and persona. But Linton's formulation, with the increasing interest of social anthropologists in sociological studies, focused attention more sharply on social structures as systems of roles (see, for example, Nadel, 1957). The work on social roles of Merton and Parsons, and later Goffman, as already cited, became influential. Some of the essays accept that, for certain purposes, 'role' can be used in analysis, as a general concept: but it is also subjected to a closer reexamination than almost anything else in the monographs.

This tone is set by the very first essay, Goodenough's 'Rethinking "Status" and "Role": Toward a General Model of the Cultural Organization of Social Relationships' (1). Goodenough is dissatisfied with the impasse into which we have run through the use of status and role as, to use our own shorthand, 'global' concepts, covering types of facts which need to be clearly differentiated. At the same time, he is dissatisfied with the present tendency to look at structural relationships apart from their cultural content. Drawing analogies from structural linguistics, he therefore attempts to construct a means of establishing both vocabularies and a syntax of the rules of 'roles.' To do this, he aims at a clearer specification of terms to describe the attributes of individuals and the relationships between them. He suggests, therefore, that status should not be, as he says Linton treated it, a means of reference to categories or kinds of persons, but that it should be confined to combinations of right and duty only. Social 'positions' in a categorical sense he calls 'social identities'. Each person has several social identities, and in specific situations one is selected as appropriate: this Goodenough terms 'the selector's *social persona* in the interaction'.

We are not, in this Introduction, summarizing any of the essays, and the preceding sketch is intended only to indicate the drive for the refinement of concepts which in the past have been illuminatingly employed, in order to secure more penetrating analysis. Having specified his terms, Goodenough proceeds to outline different types of situation in which these clarify relations between various egos and alters. On the cultural content side, he distinguishes the ranges of rights and duties, as against privileges and immunities – following here the terminology of the jurist, Hohfeld, which Hoebel has tried to get anthropologists to adopt. Goodenough thereupon proposes a technique by use of scalograms, to work out whether there are right-duty/privilege-immunity clusters in particular identity relationships as seen *by single informants*. Varied cultural demands – such as 'sleeping in the same house', 'joking sexually in public' – are taken, and the informant is asked whether each demand applies in a particular identity relationship. These combine to give specific composite pictures of duty-scales. Goodenough argues that owing to limitations on the cognitive power of individuals – here is another example of an author citing psychological research – the demands, each forming a 'status dimension', must be limited in number to seven or less. He suggests that these duty-scales can be powerful instruments of social analysis, since (as he demonstrates by examples) they will allow objective measurement of anger, insult, flattery, and the gravity of offences. The last point is illustrated by a situation where breach of norm on the part of one identity justifies severe breach of duty by another. This will lead to precision in the study of single societies, and in the comparison of different societies.

This summary does not set out all the intricacies of the argument; but we have discussed this essay in order to illustrate what we mean when we say several authors see one line of advance in an increasing refinement of established concepts, and specification of others, to replace single concepts which, in their traditional global form, have outlived their usefulness. Goodenough's essay is the most explicit treatment of 'status' and 'role' in this way; but it seems to us that similar procedures are at least implicit in those parts of Lloyd's and Southall's essays on political systems (2) which aim to relate changes in role patterns with changes in macroscopic political structures. The explicit reformulation of the ideas involved in social roles emerges again in Frankenberg's essay (4) on changes in roles with 'movement' from British rural areas, through villages and small towns, into cities. Like Goodenough, he concerns himself with patterns of interaction – and he turns to cybernetics for ideas to handle these patterns. Both of them find in Goffman's

Introduction

searching study of *The Presentation of Self in Everyday Life*
(1959) and *Encounters* (1961) stimulus in handling the nuances
involved in the complexity of daily social interaction, as against
the more formal earlier analysis of roles in structural frame-
works.

The same drive towards the breaking up of established concepts in order to examine more meticulously both the framework
of social relations and the interaction between individuals shows
in other fields. It is present in Sahlins's essay on types of primitive exchange (1) and Wolf's treatment of relations of kinship,
friendship, and patronage *vis-à-vis* clientship (4), which have
been considered by us in other contexts. It occurs as explicitly
as in Goodenough's essay on status and role, in Mayer's article
on 'The Significance of Quasi-Groups in the Study of Complex
Societies' (4). Goodenough discusses the history of the concepts
'status' and 'role' and the ambiguities in their use, with difficulties that have arisen in applying them. Mayer looks equally
closely at the way in which J. A. Barnes (1954) and E. Bott
(1957) used the idea of 'the social network' – an idea which
Barnes advanced in its present general form, and whose importance was stressed by Redfield (1955, p. 28) in a Huxley Memorial
Lecture delivered shortly afterwards.

Mayer is concerned to clarify the different kinds of networks
and action-sets that have to be distinguished, and also procedures for measuring their form and ramifications. As stated above,
the same theme is present in essays by Mitchell, Benedict, and
Loudon in Monograph 4 on the study of complex societies, and
in Bailey's essay on committees and Nicholas's on factions in
Monograph 2. These scholars are finding that theories based on
concepts of groups, groupings and associations, and dyadic
relationships, are inadequate for their problems: the network,
and other forms of quasi-groups, which are ego-centred, are
becoming more significant in bridging the gap between structural framework and individual action. There is clearly a close
fit here with attempts to improve on the concepts of status and
role. We note here too Mitchell's (4) distinction between structural and categorical relationships (i.e. between relationships
set in associations and institutions, and relationships based on
common atrtibutes, such as race, tribe, and class).

The urge to clarify and refine appears also in a different context in Barbara Ward's essay 'Varieties of the Conscious Model' (1), where she considers the situation of a group of boat-dwelling fishermen in Hong Kong. These people consider themselves to be Chinese; and, Ward asks, by what model can their Chinese identity be assessed? Her starting-point is Lévi-Strauss's distinction 'between culturally produced models and observer's models. The former, constructs of the people under study themselves, he calls conscious models; the latter, unconscious, models'. Ward argues that to understand her field situation, she had to take into account several conscious models – that of Chinese society held by Chinese literati, that of the group under study held by themselves, those of this group held by other groups of Chinese – as well as the unconscious, the anthropologist's, model. She examines the relationship between these models, as set in the context of different areas of Chinese society, to assess where 'the uniformity and continuity of the traditional Chinese social system' lay; and she finds it in family structures.

The demand for rethinking, clarification, and refinement runs through all the essays in Monograph 1, that on 'models'. We have cited it from the essays by Goodenough, Sahlins, and Ward. It appears as strikingly in the other essays: by Ioan Lewis on 'Problems in the Comparative Study of Unilineal Descent' and David Schneider on 'Some Muddles in the Models'. Lewis argues that if correlations are to be established in comparative work, it is necessary to measure the intensity of such a principle as unilineal descent. He attempts to do this by applying various criteria to four patrilineal societies. He comes to the conclusion after his survey that by these principles involved in unilineal descent, various societies scale differently, and hence he suggests that this kind of classification is difficult and probably unfruitful. He argues that the functional significance of descent varies too much, hence canons of descent may not be fruitful criteria. 'The lumping together of societies on the basis of patriliny or matriliny alone can only lead to confusion. The functional implications of descent are much more significant than whether descent is traced in the patri – or matri-line' – an argument advanced by Leach in *Rethinking Anthropology* (1961).

Introduction

Since Lewis does not suggest alternative criteria, we take his essay to be an example of that important class of work which aims to prove that a particular line of research is fruitless. The implications of the final sentence are clear: more refined, multiple variables must be sought.

Schneider's essay is much more difficult to delineate. It deals with a heated controversy between anthropologists about relationships of descent, and relationships of marriage or alliance. The argument is complex, and difficult to follow without detailed knowledge of the background literature which is discussed – and at least one of us, a political anthropologist, frankly confesses his difficulties here. Nevertheless, for present purposes it is clear that Schneider is trying to clarify the terminological and other muddles that he considers obstruct agreement: he points out to the contestants where they are talking in fact about different things, when they appear to be talking about the same thing. For, he says, there are two categories of anthropologists involved, and though there may be differences between the members of each category, they are distinctive from the others. There are the descent theory anthropologists (Fortes, Gluckman, Goody), who look for actual groups of people who intermarry with one another, and alliance theory anthropologists (Lévi-Strauss, Leach, Needham), who are primarily interested in 'that construct or model which is fabricated by the anthropologist and which is presumed to have, as its concrete expression, the norms for social relations and the rules governing the constitution of social groups and their interrelations'. Schneider argues that aside from weaknesses in each theory, they both contain contradictions and obscurities in their formulations. Most of the disputants are not clear in their arguments with one another on how far they are erecting conceptual models, which do not refer to real segments of the society, and how far they are referring to actual segments, based mainly on ownership of property and other jural rights. He suggests that this is because each of the theories is elaborated for a different type of society. The alliance theory is formulated for systems (which Schneider calls segmental) in which marriages of women proceed always from one segment to another; the descent theory for systems (which Schneider calls segmentary) in which men in one segment can marry into a number of other segments.

Schneider feels that each protagonist is driven by the polemical situation to defend 'his type', and that leads to the 'propagation of whole-system, over-simple typologies'. His own plea is for the use of typologies for specific problems, 'not for sorting of concrete societies into unchangeable, inherent, inalienable categories'. Selection of various elements, rigorously defined, and examination of combinations, permutations, and recombinations of these elements in many constellations, will prove more profitable.

SPECIFICATION OF CONTEXT

Schneider's essay contains also a plea for the clearer specification of more limited and varying contexts of relations, in order to assess the association of variables. Similar demands are present in a number of other essays on various subjects. They appear in every essay of the Monograph 2 on political problems. Bailey, in examining the alleged value, or rather 'the mystique', of 'consensus' in committees, distinguishes what he calls elite and arena councils, the size of councils, forms of external relationships. Nicholas places factional disputes in various types of situation. Lloyd looks at a limited political problem, by classifying three polities in terms of modes of recruitment of the elite and analysing their association with four other important variables. Southall argues for 'partial analysis of partial systems', and takes as his criterion for classifying political systems the differentiation of political roles. In Monograph 3, Bradbury looks at the contexts in which Edo cults of the dead, as against ancestral cults, may be significant; while Winter, in analysing Iraqw religion stresses, much as Schneider does, that there are with reference to this problem at least two types of society in Africa.

THE SEARCH FOR THE BROAD HYPOTHESIS OR THEORY

It seems, then, that most of the contributors to this volume favour clarification, the breaking down, and the refinement, of standard concepts, together with closer specification of narrower social contexts, as likely to be a more fruitful line of advance than the search for sweeping generalizations. This is explicitly stated in a few essays, and is implicit in others. Since contributors were asked to write papers indicating where they thought new approaches would be fruitful, we believe we may assume that the essays in this series reflect the feeling of our younger colleagues, and that they did not merely submit to us essays on a problem on which they happened to be working. There was, of course, in the discussion on the papers, argument on this point: as there was plenty of abstract argument about scientific method. But it must be significant that perhaps only two out of a score of papers can be seen as arguing for a much wider treatment of a specific problem – and we are not sure that this is a correct interpretation of Geertz's paper (3) when taken in its entirety, or of Spiro's essay at clarifying the various dimensions involved in the study or religion. Both of them emphasize the close and meticulous analyses of facts in restricted contexts: their plea is rather for an increase in the disciplines whose techniques and concepts should be employed in analysis by social anthropologists.

All the essays in fact show that social anthropologists are ready to turn where they feel they can get help to solve a specific problem. But the one difference we find between British and American contributors is that the British on the whole confine themselves to a narrower range of other disciplines – those commonly grouped as the social sciences. As stated above, Loudon's essay on 'Religious Order and Mental Disorder' (4) illustrates this restriction. Turner, in his analysis of Ndembu colour classification (3), is aware of how closely his problems raise issues treated by the psycho-analysts, but he eschews involvement in psycho-analytic interpretations. The American anthropologists are readier to move outside the restricted range of the social sciences to draw on disciplines which employ quite different techniques and concepts.

CONCLUSION

Overall, then, these essays, whether they consider a single society or make surveys over several societies, show the continuing balancing of detailed, meticulous analysis of limited social fields with comparative checking that has long characterized the subject. The meticulous analysis of a single situation dominates in Turner's essay on colour classification, as it does in Bradbury's on Edo and Winter's on Iraqw religion. It forms too a core to Geertz's paper (all in Monograph 3). The comparative survey dominates Sahlins's analysis of exchange (1) and Wolf's of kinship, friendship, and patronage. Both types of analysis are strongly present in all the essays.

We have not attempted in this Introduction to discuss the argument of each essay or to assess its merits. The field covered by the essays shows that, even setting aside ethnographic specialization, a social anthropologist now will find it difficult to be competent on political problems, economic problems, domestic life, religious action, etc. – particularly as more and more is drawn from cognate disciplines. Therefore we are not competent to assess more than a few of the essays, and to do that would have been invidious. Instead, we have tried to delineate what we see as common in these new approaches, spread over a variety of problems and printed in four Monographs. Our own essay may be at least a guide to where readers can find the new leads that are being pursued by a younger generation of social anthropologists.

ACKNOWLEDGEMENTS

Finally, we have to thank, for our colleagues and ourselves, a number of people on whom this symposium has depended. Professor Raymond Firth conceived the plan and pushed through the preliminary arrangements, with Professor Fred Eggan. The Executive Board of the American Anthropological Association was kind enough to sponsor a request to the National Science Foundation which provided the financial support to enable the Americans to travel to Britain. Dr Michael Banton, as Honorary Secretary of the Association, organized the conference, and has acted as editor of the Monographs. The Fellows and domestic staff of Jesus College, Cambridge, provided a setting in which we met in great comfort amidst pleasant surroundings; and this side of our foregathering

Introduction

was admirably handled by Mr G. I. Jones, Lecturer in Social Anthropology in Cambridge University and Fellow of Jesus College. Mr John Harvard-Watts and Miss Diana Burfield of Tavistock Publications have been invaluable and generous in help over publication.

A number of anthropologists worked hard in preparing openings to the discussion of each section. Some of the Americans who presented papers undertook this double duty. The following British Anthropologists filled the role: Dr M. Banton, Dr P. Cohen, Dr J. Goody, and Professor P. M. Worsley. We had also the pleasure of the company of Professor G. C. Homans of Harvard, a sociologist who has worked with social anthropologists, and who effectively prevented us from developing too great ethnocentricity. He travelled especially from America to attend the meeting.

Finally, Gluckman insists, on behalf of the Association of Social Anthropologists of the British Commonwealth, on thanking Fred Eggan. As Firth inspired the meeting, Eggan, though acting as an individual, made it possible. In many ways, including his own presence as an American elder, supported only by the happy chance of Professor Sol Tax being in Britain, he contributed to what was a memorable occasion in the history of social anthropology – which is permanently encapsulated in these four volumes. And Eggan wishes, on behalf of the American group, to express their appreciation of the fine hospitality of their hosts which went beyond the strict requirements of the occasion, and to thank Max Gluckman for the excellence of his chairmanship and for assuming the task of drafting this introduction. To the authors of the essays, our joint thanks are due.

REFERENCES

BARNES, J. A. 1954. Class and Committees in a Norwegian Island Parish. *Human Relations* 7: 39-58.

BOTT, E. 1957. *Family and Social Network*. London: Tavistock Publications.

CORNFORD, F. M. 1908. *Microcosmographia Academica: Being a Guide for the Young Academic Politician*. Cambridge: Heffer (reprinted 1953).

c

Max Gluckman and Fred Eggan

EASTON, D. 1953. *The Political System*. New York: Knopf.

—— 1959. Political Anthropology. In B. J. Siegel (ed.), *Biennial Review of Anthropology*. Stanford: Stanford University Press.

FALLERS, L. A. No date: about 1956. *Bantu Bureaucracy: A Study of Integration and Conflict in the Politics of an East African People*. Cambridge: Heffer, for the East African Institute of Social Research.

FIRTH, R. 1939. *Primitive Polynesian Economy*. London: Routledge.

—— 1946. *Malay Fishermen: Their Peasant Economy*. London: Kegan Paul, Trench, Trubner.

FIRTH, R. & YAMEY, B. S. 1964. *Capital, Saving and Credit in Peasant Societies*. London: Allen & Unwin.

FORTES, M. & EVANS-PRITCHARD, E. E. (eds.). 1940. *African Political Systems*. London: Oxford University Press, for the International African Institute.

GEERTZ, C. 1960. *The Religion of Java*. Glencoe, Ill.: The Free Press.

GOFFMAN, E. 1959. *The Presentation of Self in Everyday Life*. New York: Doubleday Anchor Books.

—— 1961. *Encounters: Two Studies in the Sociology of Interaction*. Indianopolis: Bobbs-Merrill.

HORTON, R. 1964. Ritual Man in Africa. *Africa* 34.

LEACH, E. R. 1961. *Rethinking Anthropology*. London: Athlone Press.

LINTON, R. 1936. *The Study of Man*. New York: Appleton-Century.

LLEWELLYN, K. & HOEBEL, E. A. 1941. *The Cheyenne Way: Conflict and Case Law in Primitive Jurisprudence*. Norman: University of Oklahoma Press; London: Allen & Unwin.

MANDELBAUM, D., LASKER, G. W. & ALBERT, E. M. 1963. *The Teaching of Anthropology*. American Anthropological Association, Memoir 94.

MERTON, R. K. *Social Theory and Social Structure*. 1957 (revised and enlarged edition). Glencoe, Ill.: The Free Press.

NADEL, S. F. 1957. *The Theory of Social Structure*. London: Cohen & West; Glencoe, Ill.: The Free Press.

REDFIELD, R. 1955. Societies and Cultures as Natural Systems. *Journal of the Royal Anthropological Institute* 85: 19-32.

WHEARE, K. C. 1955. *Government by Committee*. Oxford: Clarendon Press.

Eric R. Wolf

Kinship, Friendship, and Patron-Client Relations in Complex Societies

CORE AND PERIPHERY IN COMPLEX SOCIETIES

The anthropologist's study of complex societies receives its major justification from the fact that such societies are not as well organized and tightly knit as their spokesmen would on occasion like to make people believe. If we analyze their economic systems, we shall find in any one such society resources which are strategic to the system – and organizations set up to utilize these strategic resources – but we shall also find resources and organizations which are at best supplementary or wholly peripheral. If we drew these relations on a map, some areas would show strong concentrations of strategic resources and the accompanying core organizations; other areas would appear in grey or white, economic *terra incognita* from the point of view of the larger system. The same point may be made with regard to political control. There are political resources which are essential to the operation of the system, and the system will try to remain in control of these. But there are also resources and organizations which it would be either too costly or too difficult to bring under direct control, and in these cases the system yields its sovereignty to competitive groups that are allowed to function in its entrails. I shall argue that we must not confuse the theory of state sovereignty with the facts of political life. Many organizations within the state generate and distribute and control power, in competition with each other and with the sovereign power of the state. As examples one might cite the Teamsters' Union of the United States, the Mafia, or the American Medical Association. Thus we could also draw a map of political power for any complex society in which the key centers of control – Lenin's strategic heights – appeared in red – showing strong concentrations of sovereign power –

1

while other political regions appeared as grey or white. We thus
note that the formal framework of economic and political power
exists alongside or intermingled with various other kinds of
informal structure which are interstitial, supplementary, parallel
to it. Even the study of major institutions, such as of the
American and German armies during World War II, or of
factories in Britain and the United States, or of bureaucratic
organizations, has yielded statements about the functional
importance of informal groups. Sometimes such informal groupings cling to the formal structure like barnacles to a rusty ship.
At other times, informal social relations are responsible for the
metabolic processes required to keep the formal institution
operating, as in the case of armies locked in combat. In still
other cases, we discover that the formal table of organization is
elegant indeed, but fails to work, unless informal mechanisms
are found for its direct contravention, as in the network of *blat*
relationships among Soviet industrial managers.

The anthropologist has a professional license to study such
interstitial, supplementary, and parallel structures in complex
society and to expose their relation to the major strategic, over-
arching institutions. In this paper, I should like to focus on
three sets of such parallel structures in complex societies: kinship, friendship, and patron-client relations. Since my fieldwork
experience has been confined to Latin-America and to the
European Mediterranean, my examples will be largely drawn
from these areas, and my thinking will be based largely on these
examples. I shall indicate where I think it could be extended to
other areas, but I shall expect to hear that they cannot be
applied universally.

We must not, of course, picture the structures of complex
society as an ordered anarchy. The informal structures of which
I have spoken are supplementary to the system: they operate
and exist by virtue of its existence, which is logically, if not
temporally, prior to them. Allow me to make use of Lewis
Henry Morgan's dichotomy of *societas* and *civitas* to clarify my
meaning. In *societas*, the principle of kinship embodies all or
most strategic relations; in *civitas*, relations of political economy
and ideology guide and curtail the functions of kinship. Let me
caution that this is true more of kinship functions than of

kinship form. Indeed we are learning a great deal about just how far or how little kinship mechanisms can be stretched and bent to accommodate different interests. Nevertheless we must recognize a polarity in function. Relations may still have kinship form, but no longer primarily kinship functions. Take, for example, the corporate patrilineages in pre-Communist Southeastern China, studied by Freedman (1958). These units combined a kinship dogma of organization with the functions of commercial corporate organizations.

CORPORATE KIN GROUPS IN COMPLEX SOCIETIES

We may, reasonably, at the outset of our discussion of kinship in complex societies, ask when it is that we might expect to find kinship units of a corporate kind. There are two such units. One is the shallow local landed descent group, usually associated with primogeniture, of the kind which recently drew my attention in my study of the South Tyrolese (Wolf, 1962). Using a hypothesis put forth by Marshall Sahlins for the occurrence of similar groups in Polynesia (1957, pp. 294-295), I should argue that such units are likely to persist where the successful conduct of the enterprise requires the control – within one economic unit – of a number of ecological resources. In the case of the South Tyrolese, these resources would be agricultural land, meadowland close enough to the homestead to receive additional sources of fertilizer, pasture on higher ground, and forest. Division of the property upon inheritance would, in such circumstances, tend to splinter the viable economic unit into fragments, none of which could be meaningfully exploited by itself.

The second kind of corporate kin unit for which we must account is the unilineal kinship corporation which transcends the local, three- or four-generation descent group. Thinking primarily of pre-Communist China and of the Near East, I would argue that such superlocal kinship corporations appear under two sets of conditions. The first of these concerns the mechanism regulating access to land. I would argue that where you gain access to land through paying rent, membership in a kinship coalition of the kind described would offer advantages

3

in increasing one's ability to obtain and keep land, and to affect the terms of rent. Second, and equally important, membership in a kinship coalition would be advantageous in situations where the state delegated the taxing power and the execution of other demands to entities on the local level. Paying taxes through lineages or sub-lineages thus offers an opportunity to distribute the tax burden within the community on local terms, together with an ability to call on the protection and aid of these lineages. These two conditions, then, and perhaps also others which are not yet clear to me – the delegation of state fiscal power to entities lower down in the political hierarchy, coupled with the system which Hans Bobek (1962, pp. 233-240) has called 'rent-capitalism' – would favor the emergence of the large-scale kin coalitions which anthropologists call ranked unilineal corporate descent groups.

CORPORATE COMMUNITIES

I would invoke similar factors for the continued existence, in certain parts of the world, of what I have labeled elsewhere the closed corporate peasant community (Wolf, 1955, 1957). Such communities – and I am thinking here primarily of Middle America, but also of Central Java, the Russian *mir*, perhaps also the Near Eastern *musha'a* – occur in areas where the central power does not or cannot intervene in direct administration, but where certain collective tasks in taxation and corvée are imposed on the village as a whole, and where the local village retains or builds administrative devices of its own natural and social resources.

Both corporate kin groups and corporate peasant villages are growing fewer in the modern world. One is tempted to point out that historically the essential change in organizational forms leading from so-called traditional to modern societies lies in the elaboration – in the Mediterranean world – of non-agricultural corporate units like the *maone* and *commenda* which – though originally commercial or artisan kinship organizations – developed the organizational potential of the corporate business structure.

Corporate kinship organization thus occurs where the groups

4

involved have a patrimony to defend, and where the interests
associated with this defense can best be served by the maintenance of such a coalition. Such groups, too, must restrict and
regulate the affinal bond, in order to restrict the number of
people who may have access to the patrimony through inheritance. Another function served by such restrictions and regulations of the affinal bond is to restrict the number of coalitions
with other individuals that can be entered into by any one
individual. The kinship coalition or the village coalition is thus
made to override any coalitions which the individual may wish
to form, by playing off affinal and consanguineal ties against
each other.

INDIVIDUAL-CENTERED COALITIONS

In situations where land and labor become free commodities,
such corporate kin coalitions tend to lose their monopolies over
resources and personnel. Instead, the individual is 'freed' to
enter into individual coalitions, to maximize his resources both
in the economic field and in the marriage market. Increasing
mobility, moreover, brings an increase in the number of possible
combinations of resources, including varying combinations of
knowledge and influence with access to goods or personnel. The
theoretically unrestricted marriage market may thus be seen as
offering increasingly wider choices of mates, thus providing the
mechanisms for an increasing number of combinations of natural
and social resources. In reality, however, the capacity to choose
marriage mates is no more equal than the capacity to combine
resources as commodities in the market. Theoretically, tycoon
and beggarman may both have equal freedom to marry the
king's daughter, just as both are free to sleep under the bridges
of Paris. In actuality, however, we find that both access to
resources and the capacity to maximize combinations through
marriage relationships are unequally distributed throughout
the social structure.

Different potentials for effecting combinations of resources
will result in a different functional load for the marital tie and
for the mobilization of kin, and hence also in different patterns
of marriage. In the Creole areas of Latin-America, as among the

inhabitants of urban slums, we may find a minimal capacity to
effect resource combinations reflected in a predominant or
codominant pattern of matrifocal family arrangements. Among
personnel located at the apex of society and capable of great
potential in making resource combinations, we shall find
corporate-like restrictions upon marital alliances to minimize
the outward and downward flow of resources. In between, we
shall encounter a whole range of patterns, representing more or
less stable adjustments to possible combinations of goods,
influence, knowledge, and power. Thus differential access to
resources also leads to differences in the capacity for social
maneuver, a differential capacity which is, in turn, reflected in
differential patterns of marriage choice.

Seen from the perspective of resource distribution, the differential distribution of a population in terms of resources has been
called the class system of a society. Seen from the perspective
of the anthropologist interested in kinship, overlapping circles
of kin tend to cluster in what one might call kinship regions.
To the extent that kinship bonds constitute one set of resources
for an individual or a family, the distribution of kinship alliances
forms one important criterion for demarcating the classes of a
society. As Schumpeter has said, 'the family, not the physical
person, is the true unit of class and class theory' (1955, p.
113).

In this regard, anthropologists need to pay much more attention to the rise and fall of families than they have done in the
past. The best material to date comes from China, where a
number of studies show the rise of families to gentry status, as
well as their subsequent decline (see, for instance, Fei, 1953;
Hsu, 1948; Yang, 1945). Similarly, Pi-Sunyer has recently
shown how in the Mexican town of Zamora a new elite of entrepreneurs, who rose by their bootstraps during the revolution to
displace an older landed aristocracy, has nevertheless fathered
a set of sons who – in the changed circumstances of their lives –
model themselves on that older aristocracy, to the detriment of
the parental enterprises created by their self-educated and
unpolished fathers (1962). I have, similarly, described how in
Puerto Rico poor immigrants from Spain rose from rags to
riches in the course of an exploitative process, but how the sons

of these immigrants did not take up the parental enterprise. Instead, the father would send home to Spain for a poor young kinsman or youth from his home community, discipline him mercilessly in the tasks of business, turn him into a son-in-law, and pass the business on to him, rather than to the no-good sons (Wolf, 1956). Here, too, the anthropologist may follow Schumpeter's lead and ask himself why and how some families rise and others fall, 'quite apart from accidents', as he says, 'to which we attribute a certain importance but not the crucial role' (1955, p. 118).

PERSISTENT FUNCTIONS OF THE FAMILY

Nor is it at all self-evident, to this writer, why *families* – rather than some other kind of unit – should be the functional entities within kin circles and in connecting circles. If we do not regard the family as a natural group, then we must at least assay its functional capacity and range, to account for its continued persistence. One of its characteristics which continues to recommend it is its ability effectively to unite a number of functions.

There are, of course, the usual functions of economic provisioning, socialization, the exchange of sexual services, the bestowal of affect. Although each of these functions could be handled in segmented and institutionalized fashion by a separate institution, the family can perform these multiple tasks in small units of output and in quick succession, with a relatively low cost and overhead. At any one time, the demands of a family represent only small-scale demands, for a quart of milk rather than for a railroad car, a song rather than a jukebox, an aspirin rather than the output of Lever Brothers. Moreover, these small-scale demands occur in quick succession, and involve a rapid shift of labor to meet them, a trip to the store to get a bottle for the baby when the old one breaks, followed by the preparation of peanut butter and jelly sandwiches, followed by a game of chess. Maximally efficient for the least amount of cost, therefore, the family is also maximally adaptive to changes in the conditions that define and circumscribe its existence. This is especially important, I believe, in families with meager resources

7

where labor can be increased to meet variable demands – as when a man takes over an extra job to pay for a refrigerator or when the wife tends a sick baby all night – without incurring expenses other than the exploitation of self. Here we may also underline the fact that in its pursuit of multiple purposes, the family remains the multi-purpose organization *par excellence* in societies increasingly segmented into institutions with unitary purposes. As such it may have compensatory functions, in restoring to persons a wider sense of identity beyond that defined by unitary demands of the job, be this cutting cane on a Puerto Rican plantation or tightening nuts on bolts on an assembly line.

Let me make an additional point, however. It is notable that a relation continues to exist between the way in which a family carries out these multi-purpose tasks and the ways in which it is evaluated in the eyes of the larger community. The family not only performs all the tasks we have just described; it remains also, even where ties of kinship are highly diffuse, the bearer of virtue, and of its public reflection, reputation. Because the family involves the 'whole' man, public evaluations of a man are ultimately led back to considerations of his family. Moreover, any gross infringement of virtue by one of its members reflects on the amount of virtue held by the others. This virtue has two aspects, one horizontal, in relationship to class equals, one vertical or hierarchical, in relation to class groups above and below one's station. The horizontal aspect of virtue refers to the guarding of a family's reputation in equivalent relation to other people's reputations. Standards for evaluating reputations are culturally highly variable; yet in each society there exist vital indices for the relative ranking of reputations. These rankings define whom one can trust, whom one may marry. Invariably, they refer back to ways in which people handle their domestic affairs. Frequently, as in the European Mediterranean or among the Ladinos of Latin-America, reputation is tied to what is potentially its weakest link, the sexual behavior of one's womenfolk. The concept of honor, in its horizontal aspect, implies a fixed amount of reputation for each contestant in the game of honor, an amount which can be lessened or increased in competitive interaction with others.

8

Such interaction establishes one's social credit rating, a rating in which intrafamilial behavior is the final referent. Moreover, past familial behavior has important bearing on present and future evaluation. This element is sometimes missed in the discussion of societies characterized by bilateral kinship arrangements. The maintenance of a family 'name', the importance of family 'names', even in situations where genealogical reckoning is weak or shallow, make less sense when thought of in terms of patrilineal or matrilineal filiation than in terms of the storage and enlargement of virtue for each family. What has been said here of horizontal virtue holds with increased intensity for members of ranked class groups. The point is obvious and need not be labored in this context.

COOPERATION OF KIN IN NON-KIN SITUATIONS

Not only does filiation with a family define one's social credit rating. It also structures the nature of social resources at one's command in operations in the non-kin realm. Kin relations in such maneuvers possess two advantages over non-kin ties. First, they are the product of social synchronization achieved in the course of socialization. The private relation of trust may thus be translated into cooperation in the public realm. I would like to point here, for example, to the relations of uncles and nephews in Euramerican culture which gave rise to the concept of nepotism. It is interesting, parenthetically, that this relation is described in great detail in such sources as the French *chansons de geste*, including all the psychological attributes ascribed by Homans and Schneider to the relation of mother's brother and sister's son, in contrast to the relation between son and father, in the absence of known patterns of complementary filiation and matrilateral cross-cousin marriage. Moreover, such a relation between kinsmen can rely on the sanctions of the kin network, as well as on the sanctions of the public realm. Should one partner to the relationship fail in his performance, his alter can mobilize against him not only the immediate sanctions of the ego-alter tie, but all the other bonds that link ego and alter to other kin. It is obvious, of course, that such a reliance on kin may also entail liabilities to one or the other member of the

9

partnership. Kinsmen may become parasitic upon one another, thus limiting the capacity of any one member to advance his wealth or power. The clearest gain from such a relation should therefore appear in situations where public law cannot guarantee adequate protection against breaches of non-kin contracts. This can occur where public law is weak, or where no cultural patterns of cooperation between non-kin exist to guide the required relationship. It can also occur in dealings which border on the illegal or extra-processual. Cooperation among kin, for example, is important in gangster organizations, even where non-kin relations may sometimes be forced at gun point, or in political hatchet-work, in which kin relations are employed privately to prune the political underbrush. It is finally useful for kin to cooperate where access to the law would entail such costs and complications as to leave the partners to a dispute economically or otherwise deprived after settlement. The relation of kin in non-kin operations, therefore, implies a clear balance of gains and costs, in which the gains outweigh the costs only when cooperation with non-kin is clearly more hazardous and disadvantageous.

KINDS OF FRIENDSHIP

At this point, the tie of kinship merges with the tie of friendship. In contrast to the kin tie, the primary bond in the friendship dyad is not forged in an ascribed situation; friendship is achieved. If we are to make headway in a sociological analysis of the friendship tie, we must, I believe, distinguish two kinds of friendship. I shall call the first expressive or emotional friendship, the second instrumental friendship. From the point of view of the friendship dyad, emotional friendship involves a relation between an ego and an alter in which each satisfies some emotional need in his opposite number. This is the obviously psychological aspect of the relation. Yet the very fact that the relation satisfies a deficit of some kind in each participant should alert us also to the social characteristics of the relation involved. It leads us to ask the question: under what kind of conditions can one expect to find an emotional deficit in two persons which draws them into the relation described?

10

Here it is useful to look upon friendship as a countervailing force. We should, I think, expect to find emotional friendships primarily in social situations where the individual is strongly embedded in solidary groupings like communities and lineages, and where the set of social structure inhibits social and geographical mobility. In such situations, ego's access to resources – natural and social – is largely provided by the solidary units; and friendship can at best provide emotional release and catharsis from the strains and pressures of role-playing.

FRIENDSHIP: A MIDDLE-AMERICAN CASE

I think primarily here, for instance, in terms of my own experience, of the behavior of Indians in closed corporate communities in Middle America. The community is solidary towards outsiders and against the outside; it maintains a monopoly of resources – usually land – and defends the first rights of insiders against outside competition. Internally, it tends to level differences, evening out both the chances and the risks of life. This does not lead to the warm communal relations sometimes imputed to such a structure. Quite the contrary, we may note that envy and suspicion play an essential part in maintaining the rough equality of life chances. Friendship in such a community provides an escape from the press of life, but it does not in and of itself serve to alter the distribution of resources.

Ruben Reina has described how friendship works in such a community in Guatemala. 'For the Indians,' he says, 'it offers an emotional fulfillment and a means of assuring oneself that one will not be standing alone. Before marriage and after childhood, the *camarada* complex reaches high emotional intensity – at that transition in life when a Chinautleco achieves adult status but has not acquired all its emotional rewards.' At the same time, the very intensity of the relation has a tendency to dissolve it. 'The explanation seems to lie in the fact that Indians seek extreme confidence (*confianza*) and this in itself endangers friendship. They demand reciprocal affection, and it is expected that the *camarada* will act only in a manner which will bring pleasure to his friend.' *Camaradas* are jealous of each other:

11

'once a high intensity of friendship was attained, scenes of jealousy and frustration could be expected and the cycle would end in a state of enmity'. Hence such emotional friendship is also ambivalent. As Reina says,

> 'they are proud of this relationship and affectionate in it, but from a practical viewpoint have mixed feelings. A *camarada* is a potential enemy when the *puesto* [prescribed role and status] is lost. A certain reserve on the part of the *camaradas* is therefore observed, especially in the realm of family secrets, plans, and amounts earned at work. Friendship is maintained not for economic, political, or practical purposes, but only an emotional fulfillment' (Reina, 1959).

Emotional friendship is thus self-limiting; its continuation is threatened from the inside. It is also subject to limitation from the outside. Here we may use Yehudi Cohen's observation that solidary groups feel cross-cutting friendship ties as a threat and hence will attempt to limit them. He advances this hypothesis to explain the institution of the inalienable friend in what he calls maximally solidary communities, characterized in the main by corporate kin groups (1961, p. 375).

In contrast to emotional friendship is what I have called instrumental friendship. Instrumental friendship may not have been entered into for the purpose of attaining access to resources – natural and social – but the striving for such access becomes vital in it. In contrast to emotional friendship, which restricts the relation to the dyad involved, in instrumental friendship each member of the dyad acts as a potential connecting link to other persons outside the dyad. Each participant is a sponsor for the other. In contrast to emotional friendship, which is associated with closure of the social circle, instrumental friendship reaches beyond the boundaries of existing sets, and seeks to establish beachheads in new sets.

Ruben Reina, whose Indian material I have described, contrasts the Indians in Chinautla with the Ladinos.

> 'To the Ladinos, friendship has practical utility in the realm of economic and political influence; this friendship is looked upon as a mechanism beneficial from the personal viewpoint.

Cuello, a favorite expression among the Ladinos, indicates that a legal matter may be accelerated, or a job for which one is not totally qualified might be secured through the personal influence of an acquaintance who is in power or knows a third party who can be influenced. The *cuello* complex depends upon the strength of friendship established and is often measured in terms of the number of favors dispensed to each other. It finds its main support in the nature of a convenient social relationship defined as friendship. It follows that, for the Ladinos of Chinautla, the possession of a range of friends is most favorable' (Reina, 1959, pp. 44-45).

Despite the instrumental character of such relations, however, a minimal element of affect remains an important ingredient in the relation. If it is not present, it must be feigned. When the instrumental purposes of the relation clearly take the upper hand, the bond is in danger of disruption. One may speculate about the function of this emotional burden. The initial situation of friendship is one of reciprocity, not of the tit-for-tat kind which Marshall Sahlins has referred to as balanced reciprocity, but of more generalized reciprocity. The relation aims at a large and unspecified series of performances of mutual assistance. The charge of affect may thus be seen as a device for keeping the relationship a relation of open trust or open credit. Moreover, what may start out as a symmetrical reciprocal relationship between equal parties may, in the course of reciprocal services, develop into a relation in which one of the parties – through luck or skillful management – develops a position of strength, the other a position of weakness. The charge of affect which retains the character of balanced reciprocity between equals may be seen as a device to ensure the continuity of the relationship in the face of possible ensuing imbalance. Hence, too, the relation is threatened when one party is too clearly exploitative of the other (Pitt-Rivers, 1954, p. 139). Similarly, if a favor is not forthcoming, the relation is broken and the way is left open for a realignment of friendship bonds. The relation thus contains an element which provides sanctions internal to the relation itself. An imbalance in the relation automatically severs it.

13

Eric R. Wolf

CORPORATE GROUPS AND MIGRANT POPULATIONS

Just as the persistence of corporate groups in a society discourages the mobilization of friendship ties for mobility beyond the corporate group, so it also places a special restriction on the use of kin bonds to effect this crossing of social boundaries. I believe this to be characteristic of the closed corporate communities of Middle America. There the individual who wishes to move beyond the orbit of the community – or is pushed beyond that orbit – is frequently accused of actual or potential witchcraft, and thus defined as a deviant, against whom social sanctions may be invoked. This can be seen most clearly, of course, in witchcraft accusations. Manning Nash has given us a remarkable and convincing picture of how witches in the corporate community of Amatenango are socially isolated, until their kinfolk abandon them to their ultimate fate of death (Nash, 1960). The records of the Chiapas project of the University of Chicago are full of cases of splinter groups which have left the villages of their origin under the onus of witchcraft accusations to settle elsewhere. When a person migrates from such a community, he is lost to it unless the corporate mechanisms break down and allow him to resume relations with kinfolk in the village, or further migrants seek his help in the greater outside. Similarly, in the South Tyrolese village I studied, the prevalent pattern of inheritance by one son breaks up the sibling group and causes the supernumary siblings, *die weichenden Erben*, the yielding heirs, to emigrate. In such cases, contact between remaining heir and migrants is cut and lost.

'OPEN' ORGANIZATION AND MIGRANT POPULATIONS

This is not, however, the case in 'open' communities where neither corporate communal organization nor/and corporate lineal groups divide potential stay-at-homes from potential migrants. There a person is free to mobilize both friendship and kinship ties to advance his mobility both inside and outside the community. Kinship ties with migrants are not lost – they become valuable assets for the transmission or distribution of goods and services. Thus, the Puerto Ricans of San José retain

14

strong ties with their migrant kin in San Juan and in the United States. The people of Tret, the Italian community which I studied contrastively with St Felix, the German South Tyrolese community, keep track of every relative who has gone to the United States, and keep in touch through letters and mutual gifts. And Ernestine Friedl has shown in her study of Vasilika in Boetia that 'the role of kinship ties as a mechanism for maintaining urban-rural connections is extensive and permeating. Nor does a change in social status from poorer to wealthier Greek peasant, or to any other more prestige-giving position, result in a rupture of kinship ties and obligations' (1959, p. 31).

Finally, it will have been noted that the instrumental friendships discussed above thrive best in social situations which are relatively open, and where friends may act as sponsors for each other in attempts to widen their spheres of social maneuver. The twentieth century has, however, also witnessed a new form of social closure, not this time on the level of the landed corporate group, but in the tendency of large-scale bureaucratic organizations to lessen the area of free maneuverability. In such large bureaucracies as industrial concerns or armies, instrumental friendship merges into the formation of cliques or similar informal groups.

CLIQUES

Compared to the type situation discussed above, in which the friendship relation still covers the entire role repertoire of the two participants, clique friendship tends to involve primarily the set of roles associated with the particular job. Nevertheless, the clique still serves more purposes than are provided for in the formal table of organization of the institution. It is usually the carrier of an affective element, which may be used to counterbalance the formal demands of the organization, to render life within it more acceptable and more meaningful. Importantly, it may reduce the feeling of the individual that he is dominated by forces beyond himself, and serve to confirm the existence of his ego in the interplay of small-group chit-chat. But it also has important instrumental functions, in rendering an unpredictable situation more predictable, and in providing for mutual support against surprise upsets from within or without. This is especially true in situations characterized by a differential distribution of power. Power superiors and inferiors may enter into informal alliances to ensure the smooth prosecution of their relationship, to guard against unbidden inquiries from the outside or competition from the inside, to seek support for advancement and other demands. Prize examples of such informal alliances are provided by J. Berliner's discussion of familyness and *blat*, influence, among Soviet industrial managers (1957); but they can be had in any account of the functioning of a large bureaucratic organization. Indeed, paraphrasing a comment of Edward Shils, an interesting perspective on the study of such large organizations may be gained by looking upon them as organizations of supply for the cliques they contain, rather than the other way round, by visualizing the clique group as a servant of the bureaucracy that provides its matrix.

PATRON-CLIENT RELATIONS

When instrumental friendship reaches a maximum point of imbalance so that one partner is clearly superior to the other in his capacity to grant goods and services, we approach the critical point where friendships give way to the patron-client tie. The relation between patron and client has been aptly described as 'lop-sided friendship' (Pitt-Rivers, 1954, p. 140). As in instrumental friendship, a minimal charge of affect invests the relation of patron and client, to form that trust which underwrites the promise of future mutual support. Like kinship and friendship, the patron-client tie involves multiple facets of the actors involved, not merely the segmental needs of the moment. At the back of the material advantages to be gained by the client, says Kenny of patron-client relations in Spain, 'there lies not only a striving to level out inequalities but also a fight against anonymity (especially in the urban setting) and a seeking out of primary personal relationships' (1962, p. 136).

The two partners to the patron-client contract, however, no longer exchange equivalent goods and services. The offerings of the patron are more immediately tangible. He provides economic aid and protection against both the legal and illegal exactions of authority. The client, in turn, pays back in more intangible assets. These are, first, demonstrations of esteem. 'The client has a strong sense of loyalty to his patron and voices this abroad. By doing so, he constantly stimulates the channels of loyalty, creates good will, adds to the name and fame of his patron and ensures him a species of immortality' (Kenny, 1962, p. 136). A second contribution by the client to his patron is offered in the form of information on the machinations of others. A third form of offering consists in the promise of political support. Here the element of power emerges which is otherwise masked by reciprocities. For the client not only promises his vote or strong arm in the political process, he also promises – in effect – to entertain no other patron than the one from whom he has received goods and credit. The client is duty-bound not merely to offer expressions of loyalty, but also to demonstrate that loyalty. He becomes a member of a faction which serves the competitive purposes of a faction leader. 'Crises,' says Kenny, 'clearly reveal this when protestations of loyalty and support significantly show the alignment of different patronage forces.' It is this potential competition of patron with patron that offers the client his leverage, his ability to win support and to insist on its continuation. The relation remains reciprocal, each party investing in the other.

VARIATIONS IN PATRON-CLIENT TIES

We may, moreover, engage in some speculation as to the form which the patron-client relation will take in different circumstances. I should expect the relation here analyzed to occur where no corporate lineal group or corporate village intervenes between potential client and potential patron, but where the network of kin and friendship relations is sufficiently open for each seeker after support and each person capable of extending support to enter into independent, dyadic contracts (Foster, 1961). Moreover, such ties would prove especially functional in situations where the formal institutional structure of society is weak and unable to deliver a sufficiently steady supply of goods and services, especially to the terminal levels of the social order.

Under such conditions, there would be customers for the social insurance offered by potential clients, while the formation of a body of clients would increase the ability of patrons to influence institutional operation. These considerations would lead one to predict further that patron-client relations would operate in markedly different ways in situations structured by corporate groups, or in situations in which the institutional framework is strong and ramifying. Among the South Tyrolese, there is no patron-client tie of the kind discussed here. Its place is taken by political party leadership which communicates hierarchically to the various lineal corporate units in the village. On the other hand, where you have super-local unilineal descent groups, as in China and the Near East, we find the patron incorporated into the lineage, in the person or persons manning the executive 'gentry' positions in the lineage. Similarly, among corporately organized Indians in Middle America, the individual can approach a patron – hacienda owner or political power figure – only as a member of the group, and the patron then acts as power broker relating the entire group to the institutional framework outside it. On the other hand, where there are no corporate kin or village units of the type indicated, but where the institutional framework of society is far flung and solidly entrenched, patronage cannot lead to the formation of bodies of followers relatively independent of the formal structure. Rather, patronage will take the form of sponsorship, in which the patron provides connections (hence the Spanish *enchufe* – plug-in) with the institutional order. In such circumstances, his stock-in-trade consists less of the relatively independent allocation of goods and services than of the use of influence. Correspondingly, however, his hold on the client is weakened, and in place of solid patron-client blocks we may expect to encounter diffuse and cross-cutting ties between multiple sponsors and multiple clients, with clients often moving from one orbit of influence to another.

THE PROBLEM OF NATIONAL CHARACTER

I cannot refrain, at the end of this discussion, from pointing out a point of encounter with what has sometimes been called the national-character approach. When one examines the work of Benedict, Mead, and others who have devoted their attention to the problem of defining national character, one is struck by the fact that they have utilized – in the main – data on the interpersonal sets discussed in this paper, and on the etiquettes and social idioms governing them. Take, for instance – and picking at random – Geoffrey Gorer's account of the intricacies of mate selection involved in the American dating complex (1948), or Benedict's discussion of the circle of *on* and *giri* obligations between persons of different hierarchical status (1946), or Rhoda Métraux's analysis of the constitution of the French *foyer* (1954). There is no need to labor this point. It is obvious that such descriptions and analyses do not cope with the institutional features of national structure. Yet it is equally possible that complex societies in the modern world differ less in the formal organization of their economic or legal or political systems than in the character of their supplementary interpersonal sets. Using the strategy of social anthropology, more-over, we would say that information about these sets is less meaningful when organized in terms of a construct of homo-geneous national character than when referred to the particular body of social relations and its function, partial or general, within the supplementary or parallel structure underlying the formal institutional framework.

If our argument is correct that these supplementary sets make possible the functioning of the great institutions, then it must also be true that these supplementary sets developed or changed character historically, as the great institutions de-veloped historically. And with changes in these supplementary sets we should also expect to find changes in the norms govern-ing these sets, and in the symbolic forms assumed by these norms. The integration of the great society requires the knitting of these interstitial relations. As the integration of society is promoted by certain groups who draw after them a variety of others, some groups moreover set the pace and tone in the formation of the new patterns, which draw in or influence the segmental patterns of other groups. The patterns of inter-personal etiquettes of one group are then recut and reshaped to fit the patterns of interpersonal etiquettes utilized by the tone-setting group. Put in terms of reference theory, we might say that the choice of behavioral etiquettes and the direction of their circulation reflect the degree of dominance of one or another reference group within the society. An example of downward circulation of such patterns would be the spread of courtly forms in France (Elias, 1939), the establishment and diffusion of public-school manners in Britain, the communication of urban forms to rural groups via the kinship network in Greece and Italy (Friedl, 1959; Wolf, 1962). But there can also be cases of upward circulation of behavioral models, reflecting changes in the distribution of power in a society, as when the etiquette governing the relation of traditional hacienda owner and agricultural worker in Puerto Rico was transferred to pattern the relation between the new island-wide political leadership and its mass following (Wolf, 1956, pp. 212-213), or when the behavioral etiquette of a despised interstitial group in Mexico became the behavioral grammar standardizing interaction between power-seekers and followers (Wolf, 1959, ch. 11). Description and analysis of the supplementary interpersonal sets discussed in this paper thus not only reveal a great deal about the hidden mechanisms of complex society. Description and analysis of the origin and circulation of the models of etiquette structuring these sets also reveal much of the social dynamic, of the changing distribution of forces in the social body. If such studies do not lead us to definitions of national character, as this term has hitherto been employed, they nevertheless indicate the way in which the parallelogram of social forces in one society differs from that of another.

ACKNOWLEDGEMENT

Thanks are due to the Editor of the *American Anthropologist* for permission to quote a passage from 'Two Patterns of Friendship in a Guatemalan Community' by Ruben Reina.

REFERENCES

BENEDICT, RUTH F. 1946. *The Chrysanthemum and the Sword*. Boston: Houghton Mifflin.
BERLINER, JOSEPH. 1957. *Factory and Manager in the U.S.S.R.* Cambridge, Mass.: Harvard University Press.

BOBEK, HANS. 1962. The Main Stages in Socioeconomic Evolution from a Geographic Point of View. In Philip L. Wagner & Marvin W. Mikesell (eds.). *Readings in Cultural Geography*. Chicago: University of Chicago Press, pp. 218-247.

COHEN, YEHUDI. 1961. Patterns of Friendship. In Yehudi Cohen (ed.), *Social Structure and Personality: A Casebook*. New York: Holt, Rinehart & Winston, pp. 351-386.

ELIAS, NORBERT. 1939. *Ueber den Prozess der Zivilisation: Soziogenetische und Psychogenetische Untersuchungen*, 2 vols. Basel: Verlag Haus zum Falken.

FEI, HSIAO-TUNG. 1953. *China's Gentry*. Chicago: University of Chicago Press.

FOSTER GEORGE M. 1961. The Dyadic Contract: A Model for the Social Structure of a Mexican Peasant Village. *American Anthropologist* **63**: 1173-1192.

FREEDMAN, MAURICE. 1958. *Lineage Organization in Southeastern China*. London School of Economics Monographs on Social Anthropology No. 18. London: Athlone Press.

FRIEDL, ERNESTINE. 1959. The Role of Kinship in the Transmission of National Culture to Rural Villages in Mainland Greece. *American Anthropologist* **61**: 30-38.

GORER, GEOFFREY. 1948. *The American People*. New York: Norton.

HSU, FRANCIS L. K. 1948. *Under the Ancestors' Shadow: Chinese Culture and Personality*. New York: Columbia University Press.

KENNY, MICHAEL. 1962. *A Spanish Tapestry: Town and Country in Castile*. Bloomington: University of Indiana Press.

MÉTRAUX, RHODA. 1954. Themes in French Culture. In Rhoda Métraux & Margaret Mead (eds.), *Themes in French Culture: A Preface to a Study of French Community*. Hoover Institute Series, D: Communities, No. 1. Stanford: Stanford University Press, pp. 1-65.

NASH, MANNING, 1960. Witchcraft as Social Process in a Tzeltal Community. *América Indígena* **20**: 121-126.

PI-SUNYER, ORIOL. 1962. Personal communication.

PITT-RIVERS, JULIAN A. 1954. *The People of the Sierra*. New York: Criterion Books.

REINA, RUBEN. 1959. Two Patterns of Friendship in a Guatemalan Community. *American Anthropologist* **61**: 44-50.

SAHLINS, MARSHALL D. 1957. Differentiation by Adaptation in Polynesian Societies. *Journal of the Polynesian Society* **66**: 291-300.

SCHUMPETER, JOSEPH. 1955. *Social Classes. Imperialism: Two Essays*. New York: Meridian Books.

WOLF, ERIC R. 1955. Types of Latin American Peasantry. *American Anthropologist* 57: 452-471.

—— 1956. San José: Subcultures of a 'Traditional' Coffee Municipality. In Julian Steward (ed.). *The People of Puerto Rico*. Urbana: University of Illinois Press, pp. 171-264.

—— 1957. Closed Corporate Peasant Communities in Mesoamerica and Central Java. *Southwestern Journal of Anthropology* 13: 1-18.

—— 1959. *Sons of the Shaking Earth*. Chicago: University of Chicago Press.

—— 1962. Cultural Dissonance in the Italian Alps. *Comparative Studies in Society and History* 5: 1-14.

YANG, MARTIN C. 1945. *A Chinese Village: Taitou, Shantung Province*. New York: Columbia University Press.

Addendum

After completion of this paper, I encountered in an excellent discussion, based on African materials, many ideas on the subject of friendship which parallel my own. This is

GIBBS, JAMES L., Jr. 1962. Compensatory Blood-Brotherhood: A Comparative Analysis of Institutionalized Friendship in Two African Societies. *Proceedings of the Minnesota Academy of Science* 30: 67-74.

Burton Benedict

Sociological Characteristics of Small Territories and their Implications for Economic Development[1]

'Small' is obviously a relative term. When applied to territories it usually refers to either area or population or both. In general I shall take it to mean both, but it is clear that more precision is required. In discussing the sociological aspects of smallness I shall be discussing roles, institutions, groupings, and values, phenomena more complex than square miles and number of heads, for they vary not only in size but also in complexity. What I want to do, experimentally and tentatively, is to examine the social characteristics of small territories. Are the differences between larger and smaller territories merely quantitative or are there qualitative differences? Do the social concomitants of smallness foster or inhibit development or are they of no material significance?

A distinction must be drawn between a small-scale society and a small territory. It is possible to have a small-scale society in a very large territory. It is also possible to have part of a large-scale society in a very small territory (e.g. Luxembourg or Monaco). The criteria of size for territories are area and population; the criteria of scale for a society are the number and quality of role-relationships. In a small-scale society the individual interacts over and over again with the same individuals in virtually all social situations. In a large-scale society the individual has many impersonal or part-relationships. As Mair puts it, 'Every member of the large-scale society is party to a great number of relationships, some ephemeral, some lasting, which do not overlap' (1963, p. 13).

Sociologists and social anthropologists have treated 'smallness' in two main contexts. First, they have studied the small group as found within the society. Usually this has been termed

23

the 'primary group' or the 'face-to-face' group. Sometimes it has been the general characteristics of such groups which have been the focus of interest (e.g. Homans, 1951); sometimes it has been the study of particular types of group such as the family, the gang (e.g. Whyte, 1943), or some other form of association. Such face-to-face groups exist in all societies and are not a particular characteristic of smaller territories. They will not be my concern in this paper except in so far as they illuminate aspects of scale in a somewhat wider field.

The second main context of smallness has been the particular concern of social anthropologists. This has been the study of 'small-scale' societies. Indeed, smallness in scale has been cited as a distinguishing feature of the subject-matter of social anthropology (Firth, 1951, p. 17) and as a defining characteristic of 'primitive' (Evans-Pritchard, 1951, p. 8). One should distinguish between two major types of small-scale society. Both are composed chiefly of primary groups, but in one the total social field is small and in the other it is composed of a series of interlocking similar small groups which extend through a considerable population. Island societies such as Tikopia or Dobu are examples of the former type. The latter is exemplified by the segmentary societies (e.g. Nuer, Tiv, Tallensi). Nadel has constructed the model for this type of society:

'Think, for example, of a tribe divided into a number of sub-tribes or extended families; these all duplicate each other, both in their structure and in their modes of action; each is relatively self-contained, and such relations as obtain between them (inter-marriage, economic co-operation, and so forth) do not follow from their constitution (their "statutes"), but are contingent upon circumstances and outside interests. Though such segments may in fact "combine" to form the society at large, they could exist without each other and in any number; one could add to or subtract from it without affecting the working either of each segment or of the embracing group' (Nadel, 1951, p. 178).[2]

Thus it is that, for example, the Tiv of Nigeria, who number perhaps one million, can still be described as a small-scale society.[3]

One other type of small group frequently studied by anthropologists and sociologists must be mentioned. This is the village community. Redfield has stressed distinctiveness both from the observer's and the inhabitant's point of view, smallness, homogeneity, and 'all providing self-sufficiency' as characteristics of the small community (Redfield, 1955, p. 4). Yet it is obvious that a village community is only what Kroeber (1948, p. 284) called a 'part-society'. It is less self-sufficient than either the island society or the segmentary society, though, of course, there are considerable variations in this respect.

Most of the smaller territories that I wish to consider are larger than island societies like Tikopia and more complex than the segmentary societies and village communities. Nevertheless, they possess in some degree some of the characteristics of such small groups. Chief among these is that their total social field is relatively small.

SCALE AND ROLES

The number of roles to be played in any society is to some extent dependent on its size, but size alone in terms of population does not mean that there are large numbers of different roles to be played, as the examples of the populous segmentary societies demonstrate. There must also be what Durkheim termed a condensation of society, multiplying social relations among more individuals and leading to a greater division of labour (Durkheim, 1947, p. 260). While this need not take place in a large population with a simple economy (as in the segmentary societies), it is more difficult for it to occur in a very small-scale society. Such societies may have a considerable proliferation of roles in the politico-ritual sphere (e.g. Hopi, Yap) but they have very little specialization of economic and technical roles. Thus it is not only in the numbers of roles but also in the kinds of role that small-scale societies differ from those of larger scale.

G. and M. Wilson, in discussing criteria of scale, state: 'A Bushman, we maintain, is as dependent on his fellows as an Englishman, but the Englishman depends upon many more people than does the Bushman' (1945, p. 25). Yet it is obvious that there is a difference in quality in the dependence of the

Bushman and of the Englishman on his fellows. The Wilsons describe this as a difference of intensity of relations, the intensity of the Englishman's relations being 'more spread out'.[4] I believe we can carry the analysis further than this, by looking more closely at the nature of the roles themselves. Not only are there fewer roles in a small-scale society, but because of the smallness of the total social field many roles are played by relatively few individuals. It is a commonplace in anthropological studies of small communities that economic, political, religious, and kinship systems are very often congruent or nearly so. The same individuals are brought into contact over and over again in various activities. 'Different types of primary groups tend to coincide or overlap in large measure' (Firth, 1951, p. 47). Relationships are what Gluckman calls 'multiplex' in that 'nearly every social relationship serves many interests' (1955, pp. 18-19). Parsons (1939, 1951) has characterized such role-relationships, which he terms 'particularistic', as being affectively charged. There are strong positive or negative attitudes between persons involved in them. They also extend over a considerable time-span. Such roles are usually ascriptive. The standards of judgement in the role depend on *who* the person is rather than what he does. They are characterized by personal relations.

This model can be contrasted with a model stressing impersonal relations. Parsons terms such role-relationships 'universalistic' because they are based on more or less fixed standards and criteria. The incumbent of such a role treats all others with whom he comes in contact in this role-relationship in terms of universal categories. A shopkeeper should treat all his customers alike or a doctor all his patients. The roles are functionally specific. They are circumscribed, part of the definition of the role itself. The relationship, at least ideally in terms of a model, is affectively neutral. It also has a very limited time-span, even though it may be repeated at intervals. The standards of judgement are based on criteria of achievement, *what* a person does rather than who he is. It is performance and efficiency, not hereditary qualities, that are relevant. These are polar models and it is obvious that both sets of features are characteristic of most role-relationships which could be placed along a continuum. Role-relationships change over time. As the same individuals continue to interact in the same roles, the relationship moves from the impersonal toward the personal pole.

In a small-scale society, where the total social field is small, relationships tend toward the personal pole. It matters very much more who a man is than what he does. There are strong positive and negative attitudes in the role-relationships in the business and professional and governmental complexes based not mainly on role-performances as shop assistants, doctors, and clerks but on family and friendship connections. Occupational roles become diffuse when they have to be looked at in terms of kinship connections and influence in other spheres of activity.

SCALE, VALUES, AND ALTERNATIVES

Personal and impersonal role-relationships involve values, in that an actor playing a role based on impersonal criteria is using one set of values, e.g. whether a customer owes one money; whereas the same actor acting in a personal frame uses another set of values, e.g. whether one's brother-in-law needs the money one loaned him. In a small-scale society one's customer is likely to be one's brother-in-law.

There is another sense in which the general values of a society may be related to its scale. Where kinship, economic, political, religious, and other systems tend to be coincident or nearly so, there may be a greater consistency of values than in a large-scale society where there may be different values for individuals acting in different situations or even for whole sets of individuals engaged in very different sorts of life (see Redfield, 1941). In a small-scale society anonymity is impossible. In a large-scale society, particularly in an urban setting, it is possible by moving, by changing jobs, names, styles of life. As there are more kinds of job and way of life in a large-scale society, so there are more alternatives for the individual. In a small-scale society choice is limited, alternatives are few, and the choice of an individual may have considerable effects throughout the social structure. This brings us to the question of social cohesiveness and homogeneity. It is difficult to generalize, for degrees of social cohesiveness will vary from society to society even when we are only dealing with small territories. A society like Mauritius, with its different ethnic elements each with its own religion and style of life, is less cohesive than the kingdom of Tonga (Benedict, 1961). Yet both are rapidly affected by any major decisions or changes. A strike at an industrial plant in Britain has little immediate effect on most Englishmen; a strike at a sugar mill in Mauritius has very serious effects throughout the island, not only economically but politically. Not just a few but nearly everyone would be affected. Decisions in the economic, political, and legal fields have a pervasiveness in small-scale societies which they lack in societies of larger scale. This is again because people are connected to each other in so many different ways in a small-scale society.[5]

SCALE AND MAGICO-RELIGIOUS PRACTICES

The worship of local saints, deities, or ancestors is a characteristic of many small-scale societies. These are felt by members of such societies to be intimately bound up with the personal relations within the community. They carry personal role-relationships onto a supernatural plane. Ancestors are an extension in time of the kin group and are most intimately concerned with its welfare. Neglect of ancestors can bring misfortune in a way analogous to neglect of living relatives. Local deities have a concern for a local area. Relationships with them are conceived of in highly personal terms and offerings often reflect the supposed preferences of the deity.

Personal role-relationships are highly charged affectively. In small-scale societies where most role-relationships tend toward this pole, people often blame failure or misfortune on the evil intentions of others. A man in the Seychelles who loses his job will not consider that this may be a result of his lack of efficiency or that the work he is doing is no longer required or that it is the fault of an impersonal agent like the government. He is apt to think that it is due to the machinations of some enemy who wants his job or is seeking revenge for some past injury. He may try to protect himself and/or seek revenge by magical means.

It is often assumed that secularization accompanies the growth of impersonal relationships (e.g. Redfield, 1941; Wilson, 1945), but it is by no means clear how beliefs in witchcraft, sorcery, local deities, or ancestors are related to the scale of a society or whether and in what manner they inhibit the development of impersonal role-relationships. The expectation that such beliefs will rapidly disappear with the spread of education and scientific knowledge has been frequently disappointed.

SCALE AND JURAL RELATIONS

Maine's distinction between status and contract (1909, p. 174), and his famous dictum that progressive societies have moved from the former to the latter, have relevance in any discussion of the sociological aspects of smallness. Status in Maine's sense is close to what I have been calling personal role-relationships. They depend chiefly on birth, on *who* a man is. A number of anthropologists have pointed out (e.g. Bohannan, 1957) that procedure in native courts is often devoted to finding out who the litigants are in terms of their descent and affiliation rather than in finding out what occurred, for it is believed that an individual's behaviour cannot be judged apart from who he is. The important thing is to restore good social relationships among all parties concerned (including the judges) not to conform to an impersonal law. Because of the multiple connections between litigants, lawyers, and judges, small-scale societies often experience difficulties in applying impersonal law.

Contractual relations face similar difficulties. In a contractual relation involving the payment of money, the only relevant question is whether or not the money is owed. It does not matter whether the creditor needs the money or whether the debtor can afford to pay. If creditor and debtor are brothers or close friends questions of need and ability to pay may take precedence over the strict terms of the contract (see Parsons, 1949, p. 190). Where one is doing business with one's relatives, friends, and neighbours, it is difficult to apply impersonal standards. A shopkeeper with close personal ties with his clientele will find it very difficult to be an impersonal creditor and this may well lead him into bankruptcy. It is common in many small communities for the shopkeeper who is the principal manipulator of creditor-debtor relationships to be of a different ethnic or religious origin from his clients. He is thus not so closely connected to them by kinship and friendship ties and this enables him to be a more impersonal creditor and hence a more successful businessman (see Benedict, 1958).

SCALE AND POLITICAL STRUCTURE

Apart from external political factors, there are sociological factors affecting the political structure of small-scale societies. First is the ubiquitousness of government. In a small-scale society one cannot progress very far up any occupational or prestige ladder without running into government. This is especially the case where there are programmes of economic development. Government is an active party to nearly every sizeable enterprise, not only officially, but again because of the multi-stranded personal networks connecting the members of a small-scale society to one another (Benedict, 1963). In many underdeveloped societies there are small elites marked off from the rest of the population either by ethnic criteria or by class barriers. They often have control of the wealth and technical skill (including education) of the society. They usually have a large number of dependents or clients attached to them and are very often able to control the internal political machinery of the society. Large-scale underdeveloped societies probably have a better potential for modifying this situation as educational and economic opportunities increase. In small-scale societies the elite must necessarily be small. Opportunities for upward mobility are limited and more easily controlled by those in power – again because the social field is smaller. Obviously, the homogeneity or heterogeneity of a society is important in this respect. Where factions form they are apt not to be simply on the basis of political issues, but to extend throughout the social fabric. Where there are ethnic, religious, or linguistic differences, social cleavages may become even wider and more irreconcilable (e.g. Fiji). Whereas, in a large-scale society, political relationships are only partial relationships, they are much more inclusive in a small-scale society. Closely knit family organization, personal ties within the community, traditional bonds of clientage or servitude, colour bars, etc. all militate against social mobility whether in the political or in the economic sphere.

A word, perhaps, ought to be said about the form of government as related to scale. A small governing elite is, after all, not a peculiarity of small countries. Literal democracy, in the sense that everyone has a direct say in government, can exist only in very small communities where everyone can meet and discuss a problem until agreement is reached (see Mair, 1961, p. 2), but even in small territories, unless we are discussing some of the very smallest islands, this is impossible. Representative government takes the place of democracy in its pure form. Theoretically, a small territory with an informed electorate should operate a representative democracy very well; but in small underdeveloped territories with small elites it may be difficult for an opposition to develop. Single-party states and dictatorships are very common in small territories.

SCALE AND ECONOMIC DEVELOPMENT

Large-scale or even medium-scale operations would seem to require functionally specific roles. If such enterprises are to be efficient and competitive, they must be based on impersonal criteria of performance and achievement and not on an individual's personal ties with other individuals in the enterprise (see U.N. 1955, p. 20). The affective component must be as neutral as possible or rational choices in terms of the efficiency of the enterprise become very difficult. Nevertheless, studies in industrial sociology have shown that where attempts are made to treat individuals as instruments rather than as individuals, loss of efficiency often occurs and personal elements may have to be re-introduced (e.g. Roethlisberger & Dixon, 1939). The problems of personal role-relationships occur in large-scale societies too, but in such societies there are always possibilities of bringing in outsiders. The social field is large enough to permit this. In small-scale societies there are no outsiders. They must be imported from another society. Are there societies which are too small for impersonal criteria to prevail and just how small is too small? Unfortunately, there does not seem to be any very clear-cut answer to this, though I believe research could be designed which would give more precision to the problem than we have at present. One such question is: what is the effect of the scale of a society on the specialization of roles within it?

Firth has mentioned (1951, p. 47) that there is less room for specialization of roles in a small-scale society. This is particularly noticeable in occupational roles. Even should specialist techniques be acquired, there is simply not enough work for an individual to earn his living by his specialization alone. This has serious implications for economic development, for it means that a small territory must either train and pay a specialist for performing only a very few services each year, or import him at considerable expense and loss of time and at competitive prices when he is needed, or that the specialist must be a jack of all trades with the possibility that he may be master of none.

There remain questions about the type of economic enterprise and its relation to personal-impersonal pattern variables. The economies of small territories present few alternatives. They are almost invariably limited to producing a very few commodities which are exported to a limited number of markets. The domestic market is small, and local enterprise can rarely compete with cheap imports from mass-producers elsewhere. Isolation from markets often aggravates the inefficiencies of personal role-relationships. As the Wilsons have pointed out (1945, p. 25), there is a sense in which the scale of a society increases the more it is in contact with other societies. We need only compare Luxembourg with Mauritius, which is more than twice as populous, to see the cogency of this point. Unquestionably the factor of development enters. The underdeveloped countries, even the large ones, are socially characterized by personal role-relationships. Their small elites reach into all facets of social existence. It can only be predicted that they have a larger potential social field for developing impersonal role-relationships than the small isolated territories.

Industrialization would appear to be most dependent on impersonal role-relationships. Cottage industries and agriculture perhaps less so. But some types of enterprise may thrive on a

32

personal basis. Family businesses may succeed in risky under takings simply because family members are tied to each other by bonds other than those which pertain strictly to the business enterprise. There are limits, of course. A large family enterprise must be able to pension off an inefficient relative in favour of an efficient stranger. Whether a whole territory, even a small one, can succeed on such a basis is doubtful. To speak about a strong network of personal relationships or great social cohesion does not mean social harmony or common goals, as many people interested in community development seem to believe. The affectivity of such roles can be negative as well as positive. The intense factionalism of small communities is a matter of repeated observation (e.g. Firth *et al.*, 1957). They are no more cohesive and harmonious than groups found in large-scale societies.

Early in the paper I drew a distinction between a small-scale society, which I have been defining in terms of role-relationships, and small territories, which are defined in terms of area and population. What relation exists between the two? It is clear that small territories tend to be characterized by small-scale societies simply because of their relatively small populations. It is also clear that there are other factors involved, such as geographical isolation and economic and technological development. Luxembourg is a small territory, yet economically it exhibits large-scale characteristics as a result of its integration with its neighbours in the Common Market. Politically, however, it retains many characteristics of a small-scale society. Where there is greater physical isolation, as in the island societies of the Caribbean, the Pacific, or the Indian Ocean, the features of the small-scale society are even more marked, and this is surely one of the sociological reasons attending the difficulties of federation in such areas as Indonesia, Malaysia, and the West Indies. It also makes economic development more difficult. There is a relationship between small territories and small-scale societies because in small populations the possibilities of developing impersonal role-relationships are limited.

NOTES

1. A version of this paper was read at a seminar on 'Problems of Smaller Territories' on 7 November 1962, at the Institute of Commonwealth Studies, London. I should like to thank Professor Raymond Firth and Dr A. C. Mayer for helpful suggestions on parts of the paper. They, of course, bear no responsibility for the finished product.

2. Societies of this type are characterized by what Durkheim called 'mechanical solidarity' (1947, p. 130).

3. The question arises as to whether such peoples as the Tiv are a 'society' at all. This depends on the criteria we use to define society. There are a large number of possibilities such as common language, descent, origin, religion, political allegiance, etc. Most anthropologists would take the criterion of the widest effective political group as crucial, i.e. the widest group that could employ force against outsiders and that effectively prevents or limits the use of force within the group (see Nadel, 1951, pp. 183-188; Mair, 1962, Part 1; Schapera, 1956, Ch. 1).

4. The word 'intensity' is by no means clear. The Wilsons imply that there is some total store of intensity which is invariable for all societies, but that it has various distributions in different societies. Thus as the range of interrelations increases, the intensity of relations with near neighbours, etc. decreases (they also include intensity of relations with past generations in the form of ideas passed on, but I shall ignore this aspect). This strikes me as very difficult to prove, because we are not sure how intensity is to be measured. One could argue that the intensity of relations between spouses in London was greater (see Bott, 1957) than in a society in which, like the Bushmen, there was greater dependence on neighbours and kinsmen.

5. Similarly, natural disasters are more devastating in small-scale societies because their effects are so pervasive, not just in the physical environment but throughout the social fabric (Spillius, 1957).

ACKNOWLEDGEMENT

Thanks are due Routledge & Kegan Paul Limited and The Free Press of Glencoe for permission to quote a passage from *The Foundations of Social Anthropology* by S. F. Nadel.

REFERENCES

BENEDICT, B. 1958. Cash and Credit in Mauritius. *South African Journal of Economics*. September.

— 1961. *Indians in a Plural Society: A Report on Mauritius.* London: H.M.S.O.

— 1963. Dependency and Development in the Seychelles. *Social Service Quarterly*. Summer.

BOHANNAN, P. 1957. *Justice and Judgement among the Tiv*. London.

Sociological Characteristics of Small Territories

BOTT, E. 1957. *Family and Social Network*. London: Tavistock Publications.

DURKHEIM, E. 1947. *The Division of Labour in Society*. Glencoe, Ill.: Free Press.

EVANS-PRITCHARD, E. E. 1951. *Social Anthropology*. London: Cohen & West.

FIRTH, R. 1951. *Elements of Social Organisation*. London: Watts; New York: Philosophical Library.

—— 1959. *Social Change in Tikopia*. London: Allen & Unwin; New York: Macmillan.

FIRTH, R. *et al.* 1957. Factions in Indian and Overseas Indian Societies. *British Journal of Sociology* 8 (4).

GLUCKMAN, M. 1955. *The Judicial Process among the Barotse*. Manchester: Manchester University Press.

HOMANS, G. 1951. *The Human Group*. London: Routledge.

KROEBER, A. L. 1948. *Anthropology*. New York: Harcourt Brace.

MAINE, H. S. 1909. *Ancient Law*. London: John Murray.

MAIR, L. P. 1961. *Safeguards for Democracy*. London: Oxford University Press.

—— 1962. *Primitive Government*. London: Penguin Books.

—— 1963. *New Nations*. London: Weidenfeld & Nicolson.

NADEL, S. F. 1951. *The Foundations of Social Anthropology*. London: Cohen & West.

PARSONS, T. 1939. *The Professions and Social Structure*. Reprinted in *Essays in Sociological Theory, Pure and Applied*. Glencoe, Ill.: Free Press, 1949.

—— 1951. *The Social System*. Glencoe, Ill.: Free Press; London: Tavistock-Routledge.

REDFIELD, R. 1941. *The Folk Culture of - Yucatan*. Chicago: University of Chicago Press.

—— 1955. *The Little Community*. Chicago: University of Chicago Press.

SCHAPERA, I. 1956. *Government and Politics in Tribal Societies*. London: Watts.

SPILLIUS, J. 1957. Natural Disaster and Political Crisis in a Polynesian Society. *Human Relations* 10 (1-2).

UNITED NATIONS. 1955. *Processes and Problems of Industrialisation in Underdeveloped Countries*. New York.

WHYTE, W. F. 1955. *Street Corner Society*. Chicago: University of Chicago Press.

WILSON, G. & WILSON, M. 1945. *The Analysis of Social Change*. Cambridge: Cambridge University Press.

J. Clyde Mitchell

Theoretical Orientations in
African Urban Studies[1]

Towns and cities everywhere stand out as distinct social
phenomena in which the way of life of their inhabitants
manifestly is in sharp contrast to that of the neighbouring
countrymen. Differences in behaviour as between people in the
town and in the country have for long been the topic of study
of sociologists and other social scientists in Europe and America,
and the standard textbooks sometimes pursue them with
obsessive thoroughness.[2] Often these studies remain at the
descriptive level, but the more theoretically oriented studies
seek to determine the extent to which behaviour considered to
be peculiarly urban can be attributed to certain demographic
and ecological characteristics such as population size, heterogeneity of inhabitants, or density of settlement.

In Africa, as elsewhere, urban studies raise the same questions.[3] The problems are complicated, however, by the fact
that most of the rapidly growing towns of Africa have developed
out of the commercial, industrial, and administrative activities
of foreigners who have brought with them traditions and
experience of urban life and have therefore created towns in
the midst of people whose social life was organized on a rurally
based tribal life within a markedly dissimilar cultural setting.
Thus in the towns, as Forde (1956, p. 48) has noted: 'For the
African in particular his life in the job is divorced not only from
his childhood experience but also that of his home, neighbourhood and tribe, and the values of the two milieus are often
highly discrepant.'

It is true, of course, that towns of considerable size, outside
the Arab north of Africa, existed in the Sudan and West Africa
long before European commercial expansion into Africa, during
the second half of the nineteenth century, brought forth a rash

37

of new towns in Africa. These, however, were pre-industrial towns which had grown in response to economic and social pressures arising within the social systems of which they were a part. Studies of these towns have been used to examine the generalizations developed by theorists such as Wirth (1938) on the basis of experience of American and European towns. This is possible because they provide the opportunity for testing the hypothesis that the features of the social system that may be characterized as specifically urban are due to the factors of economic differentiation, heterogeneity, and mobility rather than the whole cultural complex of which they appear to be an integral part (Miner, 1953; Sjoberg, 1960).

This may be a perfectly justifiable procedure but the hard facts are, as Balandier (1956, p. 497) points out, that most thriving African towns have come into being or are expanding today because of modern commercial and industrial enterprise depending on international trade. The influence of Western economic and social organization, including the tradition of large cities, has penetrated deep into the African continent and is being extended daily as economic and political development proceeds. The study of the extent to which the features typical of European and American cities are characteristic of African pre-industrial cities, is therefore of diminishing significance and one which is not likely to be of much relevance to urban studies in modern Africa.

Instead, the focus of sociological interest in African urban studies must be on the way in which the behaviour of town-dwellers fits into, and is adjusted to, the social matrix created by the commercial, industrial, and administrative framework of a modern metropolis – having regard to the fact that most African town-dwellers have beeen born and brought up in the rural hinterland of the city in which the cultural background is markedly dissimilar from that in the city itself.

METHODOLOGICAL APPROACHES

The particular method of inquiry adopted in an urban study naturally is dictated by the sort of problem the sociologist sets out to tackle. Some approaches, familiar in other countries, such as the ecological studies associated with the urban sociology developed at the University of Chicago, have hardly been applied in Africa at all. The approach developed by Kingsley Davis at Berkeley, California, which is concerned with the growth of cities as an aspect of overall social and economic development, has not been used in Africa so far. This is probably because both these types of study demand extensive and detailed basic statistical material of a sort commonplace in America and other developed countries but rare in Africa.[4]

Urban studies in Africa, therefore, of necessity have involved the collection of data rather than the analysis of pre-existing material. These studies have fallen into two broad categories. In one, exemplified by the social survey, various social characteristics of the urban populations have been recorded, frequently with little attempt to relate these characteristics one to another in an explanatory way. The other type of study aims at interpreting the behaviour of people in the towns either in contrast to their tribal customs or in terms of the social situations that exist in towns. These latter studies employ what McCulloch calls 'anthropological' methods, which she says, 'provide qualitative data based on intensive "free" or "open" interviews combined with participant observation over a relatively long period' (1956a, p. 58).

Social surveys
Of these two main methodological approaches, the social survey has predominated in the past, the decade between 1950 and 1960 being its hey-day in Subsaharan Africa.[5] These social surveys have been conducted for a variety of purposes. The need for comprehensive social data for administrative or planning purposes was clearly one of them. The need to provide data on a representative sample to supplement intensive inquiries was another. They have been proved necessary because the kind of official statistics on which a sociologist can rely in countries where censuses are taken regularly and frequently are, on the whole, not yet available in African countries (cf. Balandier, 1956, p. 500). So far as studies in British territories are concerned, the social survey tradition in Britain has no doubt played an influential part. In addition to this and in the absence of an

adequate frame of analysis of urban African phenomena, the social survey – which can be a relatively mechanical procedure requiring little theoretical underpinning – may often appear to be the most hopeful way of starting a study of an urban area. Finally, there is the not insignificant fact that intensive field-work is seldom as simple and pleasant in towns as it is in the rural areas. There have been many political restrictions on participant observation by fieldworkers – in the southern half of the continent at any rate – whereas social surveys, conducted through African interviewers, have not, until recently, been beset by these difficulties.

There is a fairly well entrenched belief, particularly among anthropologists, that quantitative methods are essential in towns because the data are hopelessly complicated. As one anthropologist put it:

'The relatively simple life of a tribal village can perhaps be adequately described in purely verbal terms but the uni-formities found in urban life can for the most part be ex-pressed only statistically. In the town few generalisations of any validity can be obtained without the use of social survey techniques – taking a sample of the populations and showing the variations of behaviour and circumstance in numerical form' (Banton, 1957, p. xv; see also Southall, 1956b, p. 579).

Fortes expresses the same idea:

'. . . in a highly diversified society there will be a large number of . . . principles [governing social relationships] none of them general. In these societies "norms" cannot be discovered by inspection and haphazard comparison. More systematic methods are necessary and that means the application of statistical concepts' (1949, p. 59).

McCulloch says:

'Because of the complexity of urban life most of those who have done intensive research in this sphere have found it necessary to combine social surveys with qualitative studies' 1956a, p. 55).

But the belief that quantitative methods *must* be used in urban studies because the data are so complicated is mistaken. Social surveys and quantitative methods have a role to play in social research of all kinds and are not demanded by the complexity of the data. The argument is that the range of variation of behaviour in simple societies is narrower than in 'complex' societies and therefore the modal forms of behaviour are more easily distinguishable. It may well be that the *social situations* in which a town-dweller interacts are more varied than those in the life of a tribesman but, so far as sociological analysis is concerned, it seems that the behaviour of a townsman in a given social situation is not likley to be more 'complex' than that of a tribesman in a rural situation. Is the relationship of a man to his wife more complicated in the town than it is in the rural area, for example? In many ways it may be simpler because it is hedged about with fewer relationships with affines and ritual practices. In fact, from one point of view, since social relationships in tribal areas are more likely to be 'multiplex', it may be that from an analytical point of view they are more 'complex' and hence more difficult to analyse.

The apparent complexity of social phenomena frequently bespeaks a lack of theoretical concepts available for their analysis. From this point of view segmentary societies were 'complex' until a set of analytical concepts incorporated in the idea of 'lineage' became available with which to order the phenomena observed. Similarly Dahomean marriage was a 'complex' phenomenon until Mrs Bohannan's theoretical analysis simplified it for us. It is possible that the apparent complexity of social phenomena in African urban areas is due simply to the fact that we do not as yet have the perspective with which to view these phenomena and bring them into focus. This perspective can come only when we have both the accumulation of data on urban populations and analytical effort applied to these to produce the simplification which is the characteristic of good theory.

Social surveys are one of the means to this end. The categories of quantification in them, however, should be determined by prior theoretical analysis. The findings which emerge from these surveys may then be used to test the generaliⱱy of hypotheses developed because social surveys are based – or should be based – on samples so selected as to make their findings applicable to the whole population from which the sample is drawn. Quantitative methods may thus be used to refine and deepen the generalizations which have been derived from other methods or to bring to light regularities which might otherwise have escaped notice. Thus the partial coincidence of social status with tribe in Livingstone (McCulloch, 1956b, p. 50), the greater-than-chance frequency of tribal in-marriages on the Copperbelt (Mitchell, 1957b), and the association of the greater tribal heterogeneity and dispersion with social status in the African suburbs of Stanleyville (Pons, 1956b), have all emerged from the findings of social surveys.

The use of quantitative methods in this way is not peculiar to urban studies: they are increasingly being used in tribal studies as well. As Fortes puts it:

'The value of statistical methods, of however elementary a nature, for the study of so-called simple societies has also been demonstrated by anthropologists, but it is not generally accepted that they are essential for the study of social structure in all societies and that in fact they are nothing more than a refinement of the crude methods of comparison and induction commonly used' (1949, p. 59).

Intensive studies
Quantitative methods may be used in two ways. They may be used to throw up associations of social characteristics which call for some sociological explanation, as, for example, the high masculinity rate among migrants who have come a long distance to the mining towns of the Copperbelt. They may also be used to test and refine hypotheses derived by intensive studies such as the verifying, by the use of a suitable questionnaire, of the social distance between tribes.

In this interaction between intensive and quantitative research it is likely that fruitful hypotheses will arise most frequently out of the insights acquired in intensive studies. The appropriate role for quantitative research is to test and refine these hypotheses rather than to generate them. It is thus not surprising that the conference of urban research workers at Abidjan in 1954 – in the middle of the period when the weight of urban research in Subsaharan Africa was heavily quantitative – should have pleaded for 'intensive enquiry into cultural patterning and social institutions' (Forde, 1956, p. 41), and for a 'structural approach' to such problems as the factors affecting the propensity for urban migration, the degree of residential stability, the degree or causes of economic insecurity; the character and conditions of the emergence of new social and material goals in different categories of the population (ibid., p. 47).

URBAN STUDIES AND SOCIAL CHANGE

Intensive studies of towns in Subsaharan Africa have concentrated particularly on the contrast between tribal life on the one hand and urban life on the other. Towns have come to be seen as the centres through which cultural innovations are introduced into the region within which they are situated, no doubt because of the cultural discontinuity between modern African towns and the regions in which they are rooted.

Undoubtedly colonization and subsequent industrial and commercial developments have introduced many innovations into the life of African peoples and one of these is the rapid growth of towns. It is true also that patterns of behaviour have arisen in towns which are different from those in the tribal areas from which most of the townsmen have only recently come. Hence it is not surprising that many urban studies in Africa make the assumption that they are necessarily studies of social change.[6]

But it is evident that we are dealing here with changes of different sorts and these should be kept separate analytically. Southall (1961a, p. 18) drew attention to this point when he argued: 'It is important to distinguish the rapidity of change in a system or a situation from the rapidity of change in persons.' What is implied here is that we may view the social systems operating in towns and tribal areas as relatively stable and enduring though each is distinct from the other. An individual who migrates from a tribal area into a town will find that his

43

behaviour, appropriate to rural circumstances, is out of place in town and he must therefore adopt new customs and habits. Mayer has made the same observation. Referring to 'School' migrants he writes: 'A man can easily begin to practice "town ways" for the benefit of his friend in East London, yet shed them for the benefit of his more orthodox-minded friends at home, because there is no active relationship between these two sets of people' (Mayer, 1961, p. 290). Southall (1961a, p. 19) pithily comments: 'The switch of action patterns from the rural to the urban set of objectives is as rapid as the migrant's journey to town.'

At the same time the different social systems of town and country are themselves slowly changing. Therefore in observing the behaviour of individuals in town the sociologist is in fact observing different types of change simultaneously. One such change is due to the different behaviour a tribal person must adopt as he participates in urban institutions and is involved in urban structures. Another is the change which is proceeding as new institutions and patterns develop out of old. Southall (1961a, p. 19) writes:

'So there are both gradual and sudden changes in the norms of migrant workers while the set of norms operative in an urban situation changes gradually, picked up afresh by every migrant on arrival and reverting to latency for him each time he returns to the country. The impact of each migrant on the urban situation is infinitesimal yet this situation and its norms change under the collective impact of migrants, their objectives and the reactions which they set up in [an] urban situation.'

I have suggested that the overall changes in the social system should be called 'historical' or 'processive' change, while the changes in behaviour following participation in different social systems should be called 'situational change' (Mitchell, 1962a, p. 128). This is analogous to what Mayer (1962, p. 579) called 'one-way' as against 'alternation' models of change. This distinction is also implied though not explicitly stated by Gluckman (1961a, p. 70): 'The urbanized African is outside the tribe, but

44

not beyond the influence of the tribe. Correspondingly when a man returns from the towns into the political area of his tribe he is tribalized again – de-urbanized – though not beyond the influence of the town.'

When a research worker observes behaviour in town with a background of rural patterns in mind he perceives the two types of change in one context and it is difficult to separate one from the other. Many anthropologists working in towns thus tend to formulate their problems in terms of general theories of social change which are usually inappropriate.

The clearest example of this type of approach is in those urban studies which formulate their problems in terms of 'detribalization' or 'westernization' or simply 'acculturation' in general.[7] These studies work with the concept of a 'culture' which is undergoing contact with resulting detribalization of individuals. The objections to the use of concepts like 'detribalization because of hidden value-judgements are well known and need not be repeated.[8] In the terms of point of view presented here, the theoretical weakness is that situational change is confused with processive change. Customs and values in tribal areas are part of a particular social context and cannot be compared with their counterparts in urban areas where they fall into another context.

An outstanding example is Hellmann's pioneering work done a generation ago when anthropology was very heavily influenced by Malinowski's idea of 'culture contact'. But the same confusion pervades more recent anthropological studies in urban areas. An example is Powdermaker's study of social change and the imagery and values of African teenagers on the Copperbelt. In an informative paper on the images which African scholars have about contemporary life in Northern Rhodesia, she writes: 'It appears to be very important to these Africans in a rapidly changing world, increasingly complicated and broad in scope, to be able to count on the help of kindred and friends' (Powdermaker, 1956, p. 809). Although she admits that these young people pointed out how important it was for them to have kinsfolk and friends in other towns to support them when they went there either for sports or dances or to look for a job, she considers this as being insufficient explanation and goes on to

45

say: 'Concepts of interpersonal relations are part of a moral order in which these young people have been reared, and a moral order usually changes much more slowly than the technical one' (ibid.). It could be argued, however, that the value her respondents placed on kinship and friendship in towns was simply the reaction to a social situation in which the vast majority of their contacts were with strangers. In other words, the connection between the changing world and the attitude of the African teenagers to kinship and friendship does not seem to be demonstrated. I think Powdermaker has tried to explain what appears to be a phenomenon of situational change in terms of historical change and she does this because her assumption is that urban phenomena are *necessarily* problems of processive change. This is shown in the opening sentence of her paper, which reads: 'In any society undergoing rapid technological and social change such as is occurring on the Copperbelt of Northern Rhodesia young people form an interesting focus for the study of social change' (ibid., p. 783).

One of the leading American urban sociologists, Kingsley Davis, and his collaborator apparently are similarly confused when they write:

'[The] sudden juxtaposition of 20th-century cities and extremely primitive cultures (virtually stone-age in their organization and technology) give rise in some respects to a sharper rural-urban contrast than can be found anywhere else in the world. It is the contrast between neolithic cultures on the one hand and industrial culture on the other, not mitigated by intervening centuries of socio-cultural evolution but juxtaposed and mixed all at once. It follows that the flow of migrants from countryside to city in Africa corresponds to a rapid transition telescoping several millennia into a short span' (Davis & Hertz, 1954).

The confusion of situational with processive change is not always as palpable as this. Some research workers fall into this error through comparing, implicitly or explicitly, urban social structures with their rural counterparts. The paper by Baker and Bird (1959), is an example where the status of women in lineage systems is compared with the position of women in

46

towns as if situational change were the same as processive change.

Others slip into the error by seeing urban social systems as a restructuring of tribal patterns of relationships. Banton (1961, p. 113), for example writes: 'The elaboration of a conceptual framework for studying social change is perhaps the most important of the tasks confronting contemporary social anthropologists', and then goes on to discuss this problem in terms of the 'restructuring' of social relationships in towns. He describes how urban associations, particularly dancing *compins,* come into being in towns and serve the purpose of inducting migrants into town life. These dancing *compins,* he observes, 'create new ranks and statuses in lieu of the old ones (deriving from the position in descent groups of varying prestige) that are no longer viable' (ibid., p. 120). This, he argues, is a type of 'institutional change' which is occasioned by the introduction of new values which disturb the old order. 'People move to the town', he writes, 'seek educational and technical skills, etc. These changes entail the restructuring of one social relationship after another' (ibid., p. 122). Here Banton is concerned primarily with the nature of the urban social system and the way in which appropriate roles are allocated to actors within it. He points out, correctly, that institutions and symbols, many of them taken over from Europeans, assume new meanings and serve new functions when they become part and parcel of the system of social relationships of Africans in towns.

However, Banton is describing situational change when he states that: 'An African migrant from the rural areas may adjust himself to work in a large industrial plant in a relatively short space of time' (ibid., p. 116). The individual must adopt norms and values appropriate to his role in the plant and these norms and values would be foreign to him in his tribal home. The individual does not bring his social institutions with him to town. The institutions are parts of different social systems and the individual moves from one into the other. It is fallacious, therefore, to think of rural institutions as changing into urban types of the same institutions. The fact is rather that urban dwellers develop institutions to meet their needs in towns and these, because of their different contexts, differ from rural institutions meeting the same need in the tribal social system. An urban social institution is not a changed rural institution: it is a separate social phenomenon existing as part of a separate social system so that the behaviour in town of a migrant when it differs from that in his rural home is more than likely to be a manifestation of 'situational' rather than 'processive' change.

The study of social change in the historical sense, i.e. of how one institution has developed out of another or has slowly assumed a new form as part of an overall changing society, is as valid an urban study as any other. But these studies must be made within the same context over a relatively long time-span, as, for example, Epstein's study (1958) of the growth of institutions through which Africans achieved political expression on the Copperbelt between 1930 and 1953, or Banton's own study (1957, ch. ix) of the development of young men's associations in Freetown between 1930 and 1955. These are studies of changes in institutions within the urban framework and they do not attempt false comparison with their tribal counterparts. The starting point of the analysis of urbanism must be an urban system of relationships, and I would go further than Gluckman (1961a, p. 80) and say that the tribal origins of the population in so far as these imply tribal modes of behaviour *must* – not 'may even be' – regarded as of secondary interest.

THE SITUATIONAL APPROACH

In other words it seems likely that, for the present at least, sociologists studying towns are likely to reach a fuller understanding of behaviour if they adopt a 'situational' approach in their studies. This implies that the social relationships, and the norms and values that buttress these relationships in the towns, must be viewed as part of a social system in their own right. The relationships however, operate within a framework which, while determining the nature of the pattern of social relationships within the town, need not be part of the study of the town itself.[9]

The factors that determine the context in which town-dwellers interact we call external because, although they may be relevant subject-matter in other disciplines, as far as urban sociology is concerned, we are able to take them for granted and to examine instead the behaviour of individuals within the social matrix created by these factors. These are what Southall (1961a, p. 5) refers to as 'extrinsic factors' and what I earlier called 'external imperatives'.[10]

These external determinants, some of which are characteristic of cities everywhere, may be assumed to be:[11]

(a) *Density of settlement.* Population density imparts certain characteristics to social interaction in cities. The most important of these is the wide range of personal contacts a town-dweller has and hence the greater element of choice in his association.

(b) *Mobility.* Most African towns are growing in population at a rate which is greater than the natural rate of increase of the total population of the regions within which the towns are placed. In varying degrees migrants circulate between town and town, between town and tribal area, and between different parts of the same town. This residential instability of African urban populations leads to a degree of impermanence in social relationships which affects their nature.

(c) *Heterogeneity.* Since the towns draw their population from wide hinterlands, their inhabitants are likely to come from different ethnic and tribal areas. Urban social systems therefore have had to provide the basis upon which these diverse elements could interact. In addition to diverse tribal elements many African towns contain sizeable non-African populations as well.

(d) *Demographic disproportion.* Since the industrial and commercial enterprises through which most of the towns have been established have demanded workers predominantly as manual labourers, the tendency has been for towns to select mainly young males from the surrounding regions. Therefore most growing African towns exhibit a marked disproportion in the age and sex structure of their populations.

(e) *Economic differentiation.* Most towns, because of their population size and density, are able to support a wide range of different economic activities. This leads in turn to occupational differentiation, to differential levels of living, and consequently to social stratification, and naturally affects the patterns of social interaction.

(f) *Administrative and political limitations*. Many towns, especially in the southern half of the continent, have been, and are still, contained within a political and administrative structure in which the movements and activities of the African population are considerably restricted. Such administrative and political constraints markedly affect the pattern of social interaction both between Africans and non-Africans and among Africans themselves.

Every town probably has a distinct set of external determinants and as a social entity is in itself unique, but we can nevertheless distinguish certain broad types of African town. There are, for example, those towns which have grown up on the basis of a non-industrial and non-Western economy, as against those which have come into being through the activities of colonial powers and foreign entrepreneurs. This distinction was implicit in the discussions at the Abidjan Conference (Forde, 1956, pp. 26-34) and has been developed by Southall (1961a, p. 6ff.). In his scheme, Type A towns are the old-established, slowly growing towns based largely on a traditional economy showing a considerable degree of ethnic homogeneity. These are to be found in Tanganyika, Uganda, Sudan, the former territories of French Equatorial Africa, and British and French West Africa. Type B towns are the new towns of rapid growth based on industrial and commercial development and are usually markedly heterogeneous ethnically. They are to be found mainly in the Republic of South Africa, Southern and Northern Rhodesia, Kenya, and the Congo. The task for the urban sociologist is, as Southall (ibid., p. 13) puts it, to study the social relationships – and the values which reinforce them – within this varying framework of extrinsic factors.

Bascom (1955, 1959, 1961), Schwab (1954), Lloyd (1953, 1955, 1959), and Miner (1953) have all shown that the social structure of Type A towns differs considerably from that of Type B.

These findings have been useful in testing Wirth's generalizations about urbanism as a universal sociological phenomenon. But these studies appear to have a limited interest for African urban sociology. The basic mechanism of interaction at the personal level in Yoruba towns, according to Bascom (1959), is the lineage rather than a set of specifically *urban* factors. Furthermore, Bascom states that Yoruba towns are non-cosmopolitan and that the economy of the towns, as in the rural areas, is based on farming or trade and craft specialization within the city (see also Lloyd, 1953, 1955, 1959). It becomes difficult therefore to abstract from these studies those features which relate to urbanism as such and those which are specifically to Yoruba (see also Little, 1959a, pp. 5-12).

TYPES OF SOCIOLOGICAL STUDY IN TOWNS

The social relationships which exist within the framework set up by the external determinants in any African town may be conveniently classified as belonging to three different types. These may be labelled 'structural', 'categorical', and 'personal' ('egocentric') (Mitchell, 1958, 1959b; Epstein, 1962). We may now consider the various ways in which these different types of social relationship have been studied in African towns.

Structural relationships
These are relationships, within an urban social system, which have enduring patterns of interaction and which are structured, i.e. the norms are defined in terms of the role expectations of others. Perhaps the most important of these in terms of the amount of time which urban Africans spend in them are work relationships. These are probably the most tightly structured of all urban social relationships in the sense that the statuses and roles among workers are rigidly defined in terms of the productive activity in which they are engaged. Yet, in general, the interaction of African townsmen in industrial and commercial environments has been little studied.[12] Industrial sociologists have shown that in Europe and America informal relationships among workmen modify and augment the formal pattern of relationships among them. We would expect this to be true also

of African workers. From a theoretical point of view it would be interesting to know whether such factors as tribalism and kinship play a more important role in informal relationships in the work situation in Africa than they do in Europe and America.

In African towns more attention has been given to various types of association and 'institution'[13] Both of these imply structural relationships. There have been studies, for example, of voluntary associations (Little, 1957, 1959b, 1962; Banton, 1957; Clément, 1956) like burial societies and loan clubs, institutions like courts (Epstein, 1953a, 1953b, 1954), marriage (Levin, 1947; Mitchell, 1957b; Brandel, 1958; Gutkind, 1961, 1962a), and so on.

The unprofitability of comparing these associations and institutions with their tribal counterparts has already been pointed out. The task of the urban sociologist should rather be to describe these associations and institutions in relation to aspects of the social system in which they are embedded. Thus Little and Banton have described voluntary associations of various sorts in West African towns as 'adaptive institutions' which help a newly arrived migrant to appreciate the norms of behaviour and to build up through these associations a network of supportive relationships around himself. In the same way, on the basis of Mrs Brandel's work, I have suggested that marriage payments in towns, among other things, serve to demonstrate the social standing of the families concerned, rather than to establish rights to children (Mitchell, 1960a).

Categorical relationships
Considerably more attention has been given to relationships which might be termed 'categorical'. These arise in situations where, by the nature of things, contacts must be superficial and perfunctory. There are, of course, many of these situations in the daily life of a large town which is populated by people from many different tribes and where neighbourhoods are always changing in composition. They may occur in urban crowds, in beer-halls, in markets, and so on. Here town-dwellers tend to categorize people in terms of some visible characteristic and to organize their behaviour accordingly. This concept is closely allied with 'stereotyping' as used in social psychology.

It is an essential of categorical relationships that the internal divisions within a category should be ignored. Southall (1961a, p. 39) suggests that: 'It is rather a matter of external classification than of self-identification.' But this is not quite accurate since if Ego orders his behaviour *vis-à-vis* B in terms of a social category it is implied in his behaviour that he identifies himself with a relevant category *vis-à-vis* B.

So far as towns in Subsaharan Africa are concerned, particularly in the southern half of the continent, the most striking type of categorical relationship is that between races. This has received little attention from urban sociologists in Africa, though note should be taken here of the work of the Sofers (1955). The pattern of behaviour between races, because of the social distance between them, becomes categorical. Thus any person recognized as a member of a particular race by a member of another race is expected, on first contact, to behave in a standardized way. The European thus tends to expect an educated African to behave in the same way as an illiterate African, and an African similarly expects all European on first contact to behave towards him in a standardized way. This type of behaviour has been studied closely in connection with what those who have worked in Central Africa have referred to as 'tribalism' among African town-dwellers, Rouch calls 'super-tribalism', and Wallerstein calls 'ethnicity'.[14]

The significance of looking upon ethnicity as a categorical relationship in towns is that it enables us to appreciate more fully its role in urban social situations. Briefly, it operates as a way of simplifying or codifying behaviour in otherwise 'unstructured' situations. This has emerged clearly in the studies of tribalism in Northern Rhodesia, where it was found that from the point of view of any observer the multiplicity of tribal groups could be reduced to seven or eight major categories represented by one 'exemplar' tribe and that behaviour towards members of these groups could be defined by a set of norms related to the traditional history of contacts with the tribal groups. Among these relationships of particular interest were joking relationships through which tribes, formerly antagonistic towards each other, dissipated their hostility in a situation where open expression of hostility was proscribed (Mitchell, 1957a).

In this way ethnicity or tribalism as a categorical type of relationship may be related functionally to the sort of social situation which exists in African towns.

Similarly, by considering the phenomenon of social class in African towns as a type of categorical relationship, social stratification may be related to the type of social situation most frequently encountered in them.[15] Several observers have noted that the scale against which prestige is measured is one which is polarized between Western civilization at the one end and tribal ruralism at the other. The evaluation of prestige in this way is reflected clearly in the few studies of occupational prestige that have been conducted in African towns.

We may consider social stratification of this sort functionally, as one of the devices which enables townsmen in polyglot, heterogeneous, and unstructured situations to order their behaviour *vis-à-vis* one another. There are, however, few studies of specific situations in which 'social class' has been shown to operate as a categorical relationship through which social interaction has been organized.

An interesting type of categorical relationship has been described in East London in South Africa. There, Mayer (1961, 1962, p. 585) has described a categorization of townsmen, whose social relationships are town-centred as against migrants whose relationships are centred in the rural areas. He further categorizes migrants into staunch Xhosa traditionalists (the 'Red' people) and Western-educated Christian Xhosa (the 'School' people). These divisions are shown to have a marked influence on the behaviour of people in each category who except in the work-place, confine their more intimate relationships to their own sort. Such relations are typical of those we have called 'categorical' in that they serve to order interaction in the day-to-day activities of the African townsmen in East London outside highly structured situations.

Personal networks

A third type of social relationship to which attention has been directed in recent urban studies, is the network of personal links which individuals have built up around themselves in towns. A detailed study of personal networks in urban studies promises

to yield important insights into social behaviour in towns. The
network was used by Barnes (1954) in his study of a Norwegian
island parish and developed by Bott (1957) in her study of
conjugal roles in London families. Barnes and Bott both see the
network as a series of relationships which an individual builds
up around himself on a personal basis. The concept is implicit in
Southall's work in Kampala (1956a, 1961b) and in Pons's study
of small groups (1961) but appears to have been used explicitly
in Africa so far only by Mayer (1961, 1962, 1964) and Epstein
(1961). Mayer shows convincingly how certain types of migrant
to a South African town 'encapsulate' themselves in a tight
network of personal relationships and how this network, which
extends into the rural area, serves at once to protect its members from being drawn into town-based social relationships and
to reinforce their rural orientations. Other migrants, notably
the School migrants, have loose-knit networks which enable
them to participate in town-based social activities without
thereby affecting their relationships with their rural kinsmen
and associates. The nature of their network of personal relationships therefore explains why some migrants remain rural-
oriented and others urban-oriented.

Epstein uses the concept of network somewhat differently
from Mayer. Taking a series of situations through which a
research assistant passes over a period of some days, he shows
in them the operation of some of the salient features of the urban
social system. In discussing the nature of the network of
relationships in which his assistant was involved, he goes on to
suggest that some of the people known to his assistant also
know each other and form what Epstein calls the 'effective'
network. Others are not known to one another. In so far as
these latter know others who do not know one another, a chain
of relationships starting with the assistant ramifies out into the
town. Epstein goes on to make the interesting suggestion that
through gossip the norms and values appropriate to urban life
are clarified, redefined, and reaffirmed within the effective
network and that the norms and values established in the
effective network of people in the upper reaches of the prestige
continuum percolate down the *extended* network into the rest of
the urban community. Through the concept of the network,

therefore, we are given a suggestion about the way in which norms and values possibly are diffused in a community and how the process of 'feedback' takes place.

This is an illustration of the sort of hypothesis which may be developed through the use of the concept of the network. Mayer (1964) considers it so important that he thinks that once a standardized method of recording networks can be developed it may well play the role in urban studies (and in studies of some rural communities) that the genealogy at present plays in tribal studies.

THE TOWN AS A SINGLE SOCIAL SYSTEM

For analytical purposes we have separated social interaction in the towns into three different types. In doing this we have ignored the possible relationships of any one of these types of social interaction to any other, or the effect of influences, pressures, and forces outside a particular social situation upon the behaviour of people in that social situation.

This raises the question of the extent to which we may view the aggregate of social relationships in a town as a single social system.

Studies of social relationships in towns are usually partial, in the sense that only a particular aspect of the total set of relationships can be isolated for examination. This is a problem which concerns not only urban sociology but also many other modern sociological studies. The classical anthropological study takes a unit – a 'tribe' or 'society' or 'community' – and presents the behaviour of its members in terms of a series of interlocking institutions, structures, norms, and values. It is not only anthropologists working in urban areas who have found this sort of assumption difficult to maintain, but also those who have been conducting 'tribal' studies in modern Africa (and presumably also elsewhere). They have found that the effect of groups and institutions not physically present in the tribal area influences the behaviour of people in it. The unit of interacting relationships, in other words, is larger than the tribe.

It was in order to deal with problems such as these that Gluckman (1940, 1961b, p. 14) and others have introduced concepts such as the 'social field', which have proved useful to anthropologists and sociologists in understanding social behaviour in the context of present-day situations.

A social field may be thought of as a series of inter-connecting relationships all of which in some way influence one another. As Barnes (1954) used the idea, each field is a segment of the social system which may be isolated in terms of the inter-dependency of the relationships and the activities of the people involved in it. Overlapping fields together, therefore, comprise the total social system, though we are not sure whether the social system itself should be thought of in terms of the aggregate of social fields or whether it should be thought of as a 'field of fields' in which the various *fields* of social relationships are themselves interconnected.

While Barnes sees all relationships in Bremnes as falling into three fields – the territorial and industrial fields and the personal network – all of which operate simultaneously in the community, Epstein (1958, p. 232ff.) sees the social relationships on the Copperbelt as constituting a 'single field'. However this field, which is a continuum of relationships whose boundaries are set to meet the needs of a particular study is made up of sub-sets of relationships which are internally closely interconnected but which are relatively autonomous as regards one another. The domestic set of relationships for example, is partly independent from the industrial or political set of relationships. But nevertheless all these 'sets' constitute one field in which action in one set may feed back into the others and influence them. Thus actions in the political 'set' may influence those in the domestic. Epstein developed this a little further, as we have seen, when he suggested that the 'personal network' as part of the field may be one of the mechanisms through which the feedback operates.[16]

Epstein's concept of the 'set' therefore is similar to Barnes's concept of the 'field', but Epstein goes further in assuming that his sub-sets (Barnes's fields) are not independent of one another.

The unit of observation at the first level of abstraction out of which first of all the sets, and subsequently the fields, are constructed is the role, and the sort of data which Barnes and Epstein present could be cast in terms of roles and role-performance. A role, however, pertains to behaviour in a

57

structural position. Thus while we may speak of the role of a person A *vis-à-vis*, say a person B in *his* personal network, and of B's role towards C in B's network, we cannot speak of A's role *vis-à-vis* C because he is not in A's network. Since we need to delineate the mechanism whereby behaviour between people in one set of roles may affect the behaviour of a different set of people in another set of roles (as, for example, Epstein's suggestion that the norms accepted by an elite percolate to the rest of the urban community through extended networks) it seems that we need the concepts of 'field' and 'network' as well as role. It is important to note that an individual may be aware of the roles he plays and be able to describe them to a sociologist. But the sociologist, by synthesizing observations over many situations, is able to arrive at an appreciation of the total social field and the full network of relationships of which the individuals' own social relationships form only a small part.

It is true, of course, that in urban communities the same people play roles in different networks and social structures, and in terms of categorical relationships. One of the differences between urban and rural communities is the extent to which roles are combined in rural societies, whereas in towns they tend to be distributed among a number of different people (Nadel, 1957, p. 67). The behaviour in any one role is not always consistent with that in another, so that inconsistency and conflict appears to be characteristic of urban African life (Epstein, 1958, p. 226). It is here that Evans-Pritchard's principle of situational selection becomes relevant. The concept of the social situation was used by Gluckman (1940) specifically in order to interpret events in a community (the Zulus) which had been incorporated into a wider social system (South African society). The procedure is to interpret the behaviour of people in terms of the social situation in which they are interacting. The influence of the wider social system may be judged by observing the behaviour of the same people in many different situations. Actors impute norms and role-expectations to every situation (cf. Little, 1955, p. 232) but these norms and role-expectations are frequently part and parcel of institutions and structures which ramify out into the wider society in which the local community is embedded. In following the same individual

58

through several situations in an urban society, the observer is able to notice several inconsistencies in behaviour: the individual may behave as a tribesman in one situation but not in another. Studies of the efficacy of tribal elders in the industrial situation of the Northern Rhodesian Copperbelt have shown this very clearly (Mitchell, 1957a; Epstein, 1958). This inconsistency is possible because all the values and beliefs in terms of which individuals interact in daily activities are not operative at the same time. Instead, actors operate in terms of specific values relevant to the way in which they and their co-actors have defined the situation. The inconsistencies in the value framework therefore, as Epstein (1958, p. 227) points out, need not become patent.

There is in fact an element of choice open to the individual concerning the way in which he may define the social situation. Some situations are of course relatively highly structured, in that the roles the actors are expected to assume and the norms which define those roles are fairly rigidly pre-defined. Interaction in a work situation, for example, is likely to be highly structured. But there are other situations with varying degrees of certainty of definition open to individuals. In these relatively unstructured situations the actor is able to draw on several definitions of what his role ought to be. He may interact with a person as a fellow-tribesman, as a person of equal social status, as a kinsman in the flexible kinship system in the town, or as a personal friend.[17] The behaviour he adopts is likely to be that which minimizes the conflict he is likely to experience in interacting with that same person in another situation. In exploring these problems, anthropologists and sociologists working in urban areas are ploughing furrows parallel with all those who are interested in the 'optative' element in social systems (Firth, 1954; Barnes, 1962; van Velsen, 1964).

It is clear that, from this point of view, there is no heuristic value in assuming that the town is a single social system in which all social activities and relationships are necessarily interconnected with one another. In so far as the town is a unit, it is so either in terms of the complex network of exchange of goods and services which provides the *raison d'être* of the town, or administratively as a local government authority. But these specialized relationships constitute only a small number of the total relationships of townsmen. There are many other aspects of behaviour – domestic, religious, recreational, and so on – which appear to be relatively autonomous in relation both to one another and to the economic and administrative fields, and which in a classical anthropological type of study would be seen to be intimately interconnected with one another.

The existence of these relatively autonomous fields of activity has led observers to see town life, as (Epstein, 1964, p. 83) puts it, 'as a kind of phantasmagoria, a succession of dim figures, caught up in a myriad of diverse activities with little to give meaning or pattern to it all'. It is possible that these diverse activities are indeed all related one to the other and that there is some pattern to it all. But at present the tactics of research seem to be first of all to explore those fields of activities and relationships which can be demonstrated as being related to one another and then, when the network of interconnected activities and relationships in these different fields has been specified, to attempt to see their connection at a higher level of abstraction.

NOTES

1. I am grateful to Dr Michael Banton, Dr A. L. Epstein, Dr J. van Velsen, Dr A. I. Richards, Professor Max Gluckman, Professor Lucy Mair, and particularly to my wife Hilary for valuable comments and criticisms of earlier drafts of this paper.
2. Sorokin and Zimmerman (1929). We should take note however of the point of view put forward by E. Manheim (1960), who argues that with the increasing urbanization of American life rural-urban differences are no longer the main topics of interest in modern American urban sociology.
3. The most extensive bibliography of urban studies in Africa is to be found in Comhaire (1952).
4. Kuper (1958) has applied the ecological approach in his study of Durban in South Africa. The first part of Wilson's study of urbanization in Broken Hill, Northern Rhodesia (1941-2), has some interesting affinities with the Berkeley studies of the relationship between urbanization and economic growth, but it is restricted to one town and does not cover a whole region as do the Berkeley studies.
5. Busia (1950); Mitchell (1954); Pons (1956a); Mercier (1956); Southall & Gutkind (1956); Southall (1956b); Hallenbeck (1955); McCulloch (1956b); Acquah (1958); Bettison (1959); Schwab (1961); Sofer C. & R. (1955); Marris (1961); Reader (1961).

6. Balandier (1956); Banton (1957, 1961); Southall (1956a, pp. 15-24); Gutkind (1962c); Epstein (1958); Mitchell (1962a).
7. Hellman (1948a, 1948b). Also implicitly Wilson (1941/2).
8. See Fortes (1938, p. 61); Watson (1958); Gluckman (1960). See also criticisms in Mitchell (1960a, p. 170).
9. I am excluding here those studies of migration which look upon town and country as integral parts of one social system in which townsmen and tribesmen are linked in networks of relationships in the town, in the rural areas, and between the two, such as Gulliver (1957a, 1957b); Watson (1958, 1959); Mitchell (1959a); van Velsen (1960); Mayer (1961, 1962, 1964).
10. Mitchell (1960a, p. 171). My approach here has been heavily influenced by Wirth's classic essay on urbanism (1938).
11. See also Forde (1956, pp. 47-48); Balandier (1956, pp. 498-499); Little (1959a, p. 7); Southall (1961a, p. 6ff.); Gutkind (1962b, p. 164).
12. The studies of Hellman (1953), Glass (1960), and Bell (1961, 1963) deal with the characteristics of African workers and with their turnover rather than with the patterns of social interaction in industrial and commercial situations.
13. I am using the term 'institution' here in the Malinowskian sense as embracing both the social group and the norms and values in terms of which the groups interact. Southall (1959, p. 18) restricts the meaning to the cluster of norms that regulate behaviour of the specified kind and this seems preferable.
14. Rouch (1956); Mitchell (1957a, 1962b); Epstein (1958, 1962); Southall (1956a, 1961b); Wallerstein (1960).
15. Little (1955); Clément (1956); Mitchell (1956); Southall (1961b); Marris (1960); Mitchell and Epstein (1959). A fuller bibliography is given in Mitchell & Epstein (1959). I have not been able to consult Mercier's paper on this topic (1954).
16. See also the discussion in Mitchell (1960b, pp. 30-33).
17. Epstein (1961, pp. 37, 48) gives an interesting account of the process of redefinition of a situation when he describes how his assistant Chanda finds out that a person with whom he had worked in a political organization was also a kinsman.

REFERENCES

ACQUAH, I. 1958. *Accra Survey.* London: University of London Press.

BAKER, T. & BIRD, M. 1959. Urbanisation and the Position of Women. *The Sociological Review* 7: 99-122.

BALANDIER, G. 1956. Urbanism in West and Central Africa: The Scope and Aims of Research. In D. Forde (ed.), *Social Implications of Industrialization and Urbanization in Africa South of the Sahara.* Tensions and Technology Series. Paris: UNESCO, pp. 495-510.

BANTON, M. 1957. *West African City. A Study of Tribal Life in Freetown.* London: Oxford University Press for International African Institute.

BANTON, M. 1961. The Restructuring of Social Relationships. In A. Southall (ed.), *Social Change in Modern Africa*. London: Oxford University Press for International African Institute.

BARNES, J. A. 1954. Class and Committees in a Norwegian Island Parish. *Human Relations* 7: 39-58.

—— 1962. African Models in the New Guinea Highlands. *Man* 62: 5-9.

BASCOM, WILLIAM. 1955. Urbanization among the Yoruba. *American Journal of Sociology* 60: 446-455.

—— 1959. Urbanism as a Traditional African Pattern. *The Sociological Review* 7 (n.s.): 29-43.

—— 1962. Some Aspects of Yoruba Urbanism. *American Anthropologist* 64: 699-709.

BELL, E. M. 1961. *Polygons: A Survey of the African Personnel of a Rhodesian Factory*. Occasional Paper No. 2. Dept. of African Studies, Salisbury, University College of Rhodesia and Nyasaland.

—— 1963. *Polygons: Part Two. A Study of Labour Turnover*. Occasional Paper No. 3. Dept. of African Studies, Salisbury, University College of Rhodesia and Nyasaland.

BETTISON, D. 1959. *Numerical Data on African Dwellers in Lusaka, Northern Rhodesia*. Lusaka: Rhodes-Livingstone Communication No. 16.

BOTT, E. 1957. *Family and Social Network*. London: Tavistock Publications.

BRANDEL, M. 1958. Urban *lobolo* attitudes: A Preliminary Report. *African Studies* 17: 34-50.

BUSIA, K. A. 1950. *Report on a Social Survey of Sekondi-Takoradi*, London: Crown Agents for the Colonies.

CLÉMENT, P. 1956. Social Patterns of Urban Life. In D. Forde (ed.), *Social Implications of Industrialization and Urbanization in Africa South of the Sahara*. Tensions and Technology Series. Paris: UNESCO, pp. 368-469.

COMHAIRE, J. 1952. *Urban Conditions in Africa*. London: Oxford University Press.

DAVIS, K. & HERTZ, H. 1954. Urbanization and the Development of pre-Industrial Areas. *Economic Development and Cultural Change* 3: 6-26.

EPSTEIN, A. L. 1953a. *The Administration of Justice and the Urban African*. Colonial Research Series. London: H.M.S.O.

—— 1953b. The Role of African Courts in Urban Communities of the Northern Rhodesia Copperbelt. *Human Problems in British Central Africa*. Rhodes-Livingstone Journal No. 13: 1-17.

—— 1954. *Juridical Techniques and the Judicial Process.* Rhodes-Livingstone Paper No. 23.

—— 1958. *Politics in an Urban African Community.* Manchester: Manchester University Press for Rhodes-Livingstone Institute.

—— 1961. The Network and Urban Social Organization. *Rhodes-Livingstone Journal* 29: 29-62.

—— 1962. Immigrants to Northern Rhodesian Towns. *Paper read to Section N, British Association for the Advancement of Science.*

—— 1964. Urban Communities in Africa. In M. Gluckman (ed.), *Closed Systems and Open Minds.* Edinburgh: Oliver & Boyd, pp. 83-102.

FIRTH, R. 1954. Social Organization and Social Change. *Journal of the Royal Anthropological Institute* 84: 1-20.

FORDE, D. 1956. Social Aspects of Urbanization and Industrialization in Africa: A General Review. In D. Forde (ed.), *Social Implications of Industrialization and Urbanization in Africa South of the Sahara.* Paris: UNESCO, pp. 11-34.

FORTES, M. 1938. Culture Contact as a Dynamic Process. In L. P. Mair (ed.), *Methods of Study of Culture Contact in Africa.* International African Institute, Memo XV: 60-91.

—— 1949. Time and Social Structure: An Ashanti Case Study. In M. Fortes (ed.), *Social Structure: Studies Presented to A. R. Radcliffe-Brown.* Oxford: Clarendon Press, pp. 54-84.

GLASS, Y. 1960. *The Black Industrial Worker: A Social Psychological Study.* Johannesburg: National Institute for Personnel Research.

GLUCKMAN, M. 1940. An Analysis of a Social Situation in Modern Zululand. *African Studies* 14: 1-30; 147-174. Reprinted 1958 as Rhodes-Livingstone Paper No. 28.

—— 1960. Tribalism in Modern British Central Africa. *Cahiers d'Études Africaines,* 6 section: Sciences Economique et Sociales: École Pratique des Hautes Études, Sorbonne, pp. 55-70.

—— 1961a. Anthropological Problems arising from the African Industrial Revolution. In A. Southall (ed.), *Social Change in Modern Africa.* London: Oxford University Press for International African Institute, pp. 67-83.

—— 1961b. Ethnographic Data in British Social Anthropology. *The Sociological Review* 60: 5-17.

GULLIVER, P. 1957a. *Labour Migration in a Rural Economy.* East African Studies No. 6. Kampala: East African Institute of Social Research.

—— 1957b. Nyakyusa Labour Migration. *Rhodes-Livingstone Journal* 21: 32-63.

E

GUTKIND, P. C. W. 1961. Some Problems of African Urban Family Life: An Example from Kampala, Uganda. British East Africa. *Zaire* 15: 59-74.

—— 1962a. African Urban Family Life. *Cahiers d'Études Africaines* 3: 149-217.

—— 1962b. Accommodation and Conflict in an African Peri-urban Area. *Anthropologica* n.s. 4: 163-173.

—— 1962c. The African Urban Milieu: A Force in Rapid Change. *Civilizations* 12: 167-191.

HALLENBECK, WILBUR C. (ed.). 1955. *The Baumanville Community: A Study of the Family Life of Urban African.* Institute for Social Research, University of Natal, Durban.

HELLMANN, E. 1948a. Culture Contacts and Social Change. *Race Relations Journal* 15 (1/2): 30-42.

—— 1948b. *Rooiyard: A Sociological Survey of an Urban Slum Yard.* Cape Town: Oxford University Press for Rhodes-Livingstone Institute. Rhodes-Livingstone Paper No. 13.

—— 1953. *Sellgoods: A Sociological Survey of an African Commercial Labour Force.* Johannesburg, S.A.: Institute of Race Relations.

KUPER, L. *et al.* 1958. *Durban: A Study in Racial Ecology.* London: Cape.

LEVIN, R. 1947. *Marriage in Langa Native Location.* Communications from the School of African Studies (New Series) No. 17.

LITTLE, K. 1955. Structural Change in the Sierra Leone Protectorate. *Africa* 25: 217-234.

—— 1957. The Role of Voluntary Associations in West African Urbanization. *American Anthropologist* 59: 579-596.

—— 1959a. Introduction to 'Urbanism in West Africa'. *Sociological Review* 7: 5-13.

—— 1959b. The Organization of Voluntary Associations in West Africa. *Civilizations* 9: 283-297.

—— 1962. Some Traditionally Based Forms of Mutual Aid in West African Urbanization. *Ethnology* 1: 196-211.

LLOYD, P. C. 1953. Craft Organization in Yoruba Towns. *Africa* 23: 30-54.

—— 1955. The Yoruba Lineage. *Africa* 25: 235-251.

—— 1959. The Yoruba Town Today. *Sociological Review* 7: 45-63.

MANHEIM, E. 1960. Theoretical Prospects of Urban Sociology in an Urbanized Society. *American Journal of Sociology* 66: 226-229.

MARRIS, P. 1960. Social Change and Social Class. *International Journal of Comparative Sociology* 1: 119-124.

—— 1961. *Family and Social Change in an African City.* London: Routledge & Kegan Paul.

MAYER, P. 1961. *Townsmen or Tribesmen: Conservatism and the Process of Urbanization in a South African City.* Cape Town: Oxford University Press.

—— 1962. Migrancy and the Study of Africans in Town. *American Anthropologist* 64: 576-592.

—— 1964. Labour Migrancy and the Social Network. In J. F. Holleman *et al.* (eds.), *Problems of Transition: Proceedings of the Social Sciences Research Conference held in the University of Natal, Durban, July* 1962. Pietermaritzburg: Natal University Press, pp. 21-34.

MCCULLOCH, M. 1956a. Survey of Recent and Current Field Studies on the Social Effects of Economic Development in inter-Tropical Africa. In D. Forde (ed.), *The Social Implications of Industrialization and Urbanization in Africa South of the Sahara.* Tensions and Technology Series. Paris: UNESCO, pp. 53-229.

—— 1956b. *A Social Survey of the African Population of Livingstone.* Rhodes-Livingstone Paper No. 26.

MERCIER, P. 1954. Aspects des Problèmes de Stratification Social dans l'Ouest Africain. *Cahiers Internationaux de Sociologie* 17:47-55.

—— 1956. An Experimental Investigation into Occupational and Social Categories in Dakar. In D. Forde (ed.), *Social Implications of Urbanization and Industrialization in Africa South of the Sahara.* Paris: UNESCO, pp. 510-523.

MINER, H. 1953. *The Primitive City of Timbucktoo.* Princeton: Princeton University Press.

MITCHELL, J. C. 1954. *African Urbanization in Ndola and Luanshya.* Rhodes-Livingstone Communication No. 6. Lusaka: Rhodes-Livingstone Institute.

—— 1956. The African Middle Classes in British Central Africa. *The Development of a Middle Class in Tropical and Sub-Tropical Countries.* Record of the xxixth Session held in London from 13 to 16 September 1955, pp. 222-232.

—— 1957a. *The Kalela Dance. Aspects of Social Relationships among Urban Africans in Northern Rhodesia.* Rhodes-Livingstone Paper No. 27. Manchester: Manchester University Press for Rhodes-Livingstone Institute.

—— 1957b. Aspects of African Marriage on the Copperbelt of Northern Rhodesia. *Human Problems in British Central Africa* 22: 1-30.

—— 1958. Types of Urban Social Relationships. In R. Apthorpe (ed.), *Present Interrelations in Central African Rural and Urban Life.* Proceedings of 11th Conference of the Rhodes-Livingstone Institute. Lusaka: Rhodes-Livingstone Institute, pp. 84-87.

MITCHELL, J. C. 1959a. Labour Migration in Africa South of the Sahara: The Causes of Labour Migration. *Bulletin of the Inter-African Labour Institute* 6: 12-46.

—— 1959b. The Study of African Urban Social Structures. In C.S.A., *Housing and Urbanization. Inter-African Conference, Second Session.* London: CCTA/CSA, pp. 99-101.

—— 1960a. The Anthropological Study of Urban Communities. *African Studies* 19: 169-172.

—— 1960b. *Tribalism and the Plural Society: An Inaugural Lecture.* London: Oxford University Press.

—— 1962a. Social Change and the New Towns of Bantu Africa. In G. Balandier (ed.), *Social Implications of Technological Change.* Paris: International Social Science Council, pp. 117-130.

—— 1962b. Some Aspects of Tribal Social Distance. In A. Dubb (ed.), *The Multi-Tribal Society. Proceedings of the Sixteenth Conference of the Rhodes-Livingstone.* Lusaka: Rhodes-Livingstone Institute: 1-38.

MITCHELL, J. C. & EPSTEIN, A. L. 1959. Occupational Prestige and Social Status among Urban Africans in Northern Rhodesia. *Africa* 29: 22-40.

NADEL, S. F. 1957. *The Theory of Social Structure.* London: Cohen and West.

PONS, V. 1956a. The Growth of Stanleyville and the Composition of its African Population. In D. Forde (ed.), *Social Implications of Industrialization and Urbanization in Africa South of the Sahara.* Tensions and Technology Series, Paris: UNESCO, pp. 229-275.

—— 1956b. The Changing Significance of Ethnic Affiliation and of Westernization in the African Settlement Patterns in Stanleyville. In D. Forde (ed.), *Social Implications of Industrialization and Urbanization in Africa South of the Sahara.* Tensions and Technology Series, Paris: UNESCO, pp. 638-669.

—— 1961. Two Small Groups in Avenue 21: Some Aspects of the System of Social Relationships in a Remote Corner of Stanleyville, Belgian Congo. In A. Southall (ed.), *Social Change in Modern Africa.* London: Oxford University Press for International African Institute, pp. 205-216.

POWDERMAKER, H. 1956. Social Change through Imagery and Values of Teen-Age Africans in Northern Rhodesia. *American Anthropologist* 58: 783-813.

READER, D. 1961. *Black Man's Portion.* Cape Town: Oxford University Press.

ROUCH, J. 1956. Migrations au Ghana. *Journal de la Societé des Africanistes* 26: 163-164.

SCHWAB, W. B. 1954. An Experiment in Methodology in a West African Urban Community. *Human Organization* 13: 13-19.
—— 1961. Social Stratification in Gwelo. In A. Southall (ed.), *Social Change in Modern Africa*. London: Oxford University Press for International African Institute, pp. 126-144.
SJOBERG, G. 1960. *The Pre-Industrial City*. Glencoe, Ill.: Free Press.
SOFER, R. & C. 1955. *Jinja Transformed: A Social Survey of a Multi-Racial Township*. East African Studies No. 4. Kampala: East African Institute of Social Research.
SOROKIN, P. & ZIMMERMAN, C. C. 1929. *Principles of Rural-Urban Sociology*. New York: Henry Holt.
SOUTHALL, A. 1956a. Determinants of the Social Structure of African Urban Populations with Special Reference to Kampala (Uganda). In D. Forde (ed.), *Social Implications of Industrialization and Urbanization in Africa South of the Sahara*. Tensions and Technology Series. Paris: UNESCO, pp. 557-578.
—— 1956b. Some Problems of Statistical Analysis in Community Studies illustrated from Kampala, Uganda. In D. Forde (ed.), *Social Implications of Industrialization and Urbanization in Africa South of the Sahara*. Tensions and Technology Series. Paris: UNESCO, pp. 578-590.
—— 1959. An Operational Theory of Role. *Human Relations* 12: 17-34.
—— 1961a. Introductory Summary. In A. Southall (ed.), *Social Change in Modern Africa*. London: Oxford University Press for International African Institute, pp. 1-46.
—— 1961b. Kinship, Friendship and the Network of Relationship in Kisenyi, Kampala. In A. Southall (ed.), *Social Change in Modern Africa*. London: Oxford University Press for International African Institute, pp. 217-229.
SOUTHALL, A. & GUTKIND, P. C. W. 1956. *Townsmen in the Making: Kampala and its Suburbs*. East African Studies No. 9. Kampala: East African Institute of Social Research.
VAN VELSEN, J. 1960. Labour Migration as a Positive Factor in the Continuity of Tonga Tribal Society. *Economic Development and Cultural Change* 8: 265-278.
—— (1964). *The Politics of Kinship*. Manchester: Manchester University Press for Rhodes-Livingstone Institute.
WATSON, W. 1958. *Tribal Cohesion in a Money Economy*. Manchester: Manchester University Press for Rhodes-Livingstone Institute.
—— 1959. Labour Migration in Africa South of the Sahara: Migrant Labour and Detribalization. *Bulletin of the Inter-African Labour Institute* 6 (2): 8-32.

WALLERSTEIN, E. 1960. Ethnicity and National Integration in West Africa. *Cahiers d'Études Africaines* **3**: 129-139.

WILSON, G. 1941-2. *An Essay on the Economics of Detribalization in Northern Rhodesia*. Rhodes-Livingstone Papers 5 and 6.

WIRTH, L, 1938. Urbanism as a Way of Life. *American Journal of Sociology* **44**. Reprinted in Paul K. Hatt & Albert J. Reiss. *Reader in Urban Sociology*. Glencoe, Ill.: Free Press, 1951, pp. 32-49.

Joe Loudon

Religious Order and Mental Disorder

A Study in a South Wales Rural Community

My aims in this paper are to examine certain aspects of religion in a rural parish in South Wales and to explore the relation between religious concepts; moral judgements, and people's ideas about mental illness. The words 'religious order' in my title are simply meant to convey the notion of a natural moral order of things believed to stem from some kind of non-human entity or authority. As for the words 'mental disorder' it should become clear that, although the phrase and its various synonyms are used as though they were descriptive terms, they are in fact evaluative ones. The social context of mental disorder is presented as an example of the kind of situation in which people tend to turn to religion as a source of explanation.

EXPECTED AND UNEXPECTED MISFORTUNES

Whatever words and definitions we use it is presumably safe to say that religious concepts and actions are above all concerned with 'basic human ends and standards of value' and 'the problems of providing meaning to human existence' (Firth, 1959, p. 131). It is in relation to such topics that the anthropologist seeks first for information on the significance of religion in any society. Among the Azande 'it is death that answers the riddle of mystical beliefs' (Evans-Pritchard, 1937, p. 541). Elsewhere, writing of what he terms African 'philosophies', Evans-Pritchard says that in each philosophy 'one or other belief, or set of beliefs, dominates the others and gives form, pattern and colour to the whole. . . . The test of what is the dominant motif is usually, perhaps always, to what a people attribute dangers and sickness and other misfortunes and what steps they take to avoid or eliminate them' (Evans-Pritchard, 1956, p. 315). But in many if not most societies death *per se* is not necessarily always seen as a misfortune but rather as an expected, even on occasions a desirable event, given that a death is according to the natural order of things. Among the Dinka 'it is implied that Divinity intended that men should not die' (Lienhardt, 1961, p. 36) just as it is explicitly so among Christians, 'since by man came death' (1 Corinthians xv. 21). Nevertheless for practical purposes most members of most societies do not think in terms of final causes when confronted, for example, with the peaceful deaths of old men. Among the LoDagaa it is only the deaths of old men that are not attributed to 'some conflict in the social system, either with living persons (witches, workers of curses, and sorcerers) or with past members of the society (ancestors) or with non-human agencies (shrines)' (Goody, 1961, p. 208); similarly, among the Azande 'when a very old man dies unrelated people say that he has died of old age, but they do not say this in the presence of kinsmen, who declare that witchcraft is responsible' (Evans-Pritchard, 1937, p. 77). In the same way the nominally Christian inhabitants of the parish in South Wales do not bother in such cases about the equivalent of the Zande *umbaga* or second spear; whatever they may believe about the ultimate reason for the existence of Death as a phenomenon, nobody thinks of a very old person's death primarily in terms of the wages of sin. All men expect to die and most men do not really bother their heads about why death and suffering exist except when they are faced with unlooked-for disasters and unexplainable horrors.

It might therefore be useful to differentiate two main kinds of misfortune in terms of the relative importance of unexpectedness. On the one hand, there are misfortunes pure and simple, events which are acknowledged as the universal lot of man. On the other hand, there are what I will call, for want of a better word, catastrophes, in the sense of events subverting the order of things, events which are usually grave misfortunes, always unexpected, not easily explainable by whatever standard interpretations or institutionalized responses are provided by particular philosophies or by individual cultures. In these terms, death and sickness are misfortunes, while some deaths and some sicknesses are catastrophes. The distinction has, of course, been made for heuristic purposes and does not necessarily reflect the state of affairs in every society. It is quite clear from the literature that most African philosophies tend to provide the same kind of explanation for all misfortunes, whether they are the comparatively trivial mishaps to be expected in the course of everyone's life or whether they are unexpected and unmitigated disasters, that is, catastrophes in the sense I have described. But some exceptions to this general tendency have been reported. For example, while saying that 'Kaguru believe most misfortunes, however small, are due to witchcraft', Beidelman adds in a footnote that certain mishaps are attributed to angry ancestors or to the anger of God, specifying those, such as epidemics and droughts, which injure an entire community, and also mentioning an instance concerning 'feeble minded children born to a couple living together despite exogamic rules forbidding such a relationship' (Beidelman 1963, p. 63).

In the parish in South Wales the situation is rather different. Misfortunes of one kind or another are often attributed to the cupidity, corruption, or carelessness of various kinds of impersonal but human agencies, such as the Roman Catholic Church, the police, or the Atomic Energy Authority. As far as most serious illnesses are concerned, the degree to which they are seen as catastrophes, as unexpected and inexplicable hammer-blows of fate, has been modified to some extent by recent therapeutic advances and by increased general interest in, and understanding of, pathological processes, added to a long-standing general but vague belief that for every disease process there is at least one specific 'cure' which will eventually be found, given time, energy, and will on the part of doctors, and sufficient expenditure on research by the government. This kind of philosopher's-stone approach to the problem of serious illness does not apply in quite the same way to mental disorder, at least in the form it assumes in the public mind. Mental illness remains catastrophic in so far as it is widely thought of as incurable, unexpected, and relatively inexplicable, yet viewed as something with strong moral overtones, a phenomenon which by its existence, and particularly by what is generally believed to be its rapidly increasing prevalence, provides evidence that something is wrong with the world. To say that most people find mental illness relatively inexplicable does not, of

71

course, mean that they do not have vague and broad notions about its causes, nor that these notions are not frequently verbalized in vehement and dogmatic terms. No doubt it is true that 'there is nothing to make one suppose that vague and broad notions, whose logical implications for conduct are ill-determined, do not in fact have a powerful and specific impact on actual behaviour' (Gellner, 1962, p. 154); but it is sometimes difficult to see much consistency between the kinds of explanations people make about mental disorder in general and their beliefs and actions regarding particular instances of mental illness. This is partly because among those who are identified as sufferers by their relatives or neighbours, either because of unusual behaviour or quirks of character or by virtue of their involvement with the psychiatric services, which labels them as 'patients', very few display the florid signs which are so characteristic of the popular stereotype of the mentally ill. When an individual is considered to be mentally ill, those around him – relatives, friends, neighbours, workmates, and so forth – always identify a variety of factors which they hold to be mainly responsible for his condition; among those most commonly mentioned are social or physical stress of various kinds, lack or loss of personal religious faith, bad heredity, and faulty upbringing. The choice and emphasis vary according to the role relationships between the speaker and the sick person and according to the kinds of symptom that predominate. Sometimes there is a fair degree of unanimity and uniformity in the opinions expressed; more often a single occurrence evokes a number of different and maybe contradictory expressions of belief not only among different speakers but in the case of a single informant who rings the changes on a series of more or less incompatible explanatory hypotheses. Such inconsistencies are an example of that plasticity of beliefs as functions of situations which Evans-Pritchard analyses so vividly in relation to Zande beliefs about witchcraft.

THE CONCEPT OF ACCOUNTABILITY

Empirical differences in the evaluation of the same or similar social situations are of course found in many other circumstances. Any failure adequately to observe social norms makes moral judgements inevitable. For our purposes the significance of mental disorder as a focus of conflicting opinions, where people are more or less forced to make choices in the evaluation of behaviour and in their estimation of the reasons for behaviour, and where their actions may be governed by such choices, lies in the way in which it emphasizes the importance for such judgements of the concept of accountability.

There are a number of institutionalized expectations involved in what has been called the 'sick role' (Parsons, 1952, p. 436). Someone who is ill is not expected to fulfil all the obligations of his usual social roles, though the degree to which he is exempted from them depends to some extent on the nature and severity of his symptoms. At the same time the absolution from social obligations in itself imposes certain duties on the patient. It is taken for granted that if the state of being ill is acknowledged by him as something unpleasant and undesirable, it necessarily involves the duty of wanting to get well and of taking appropriate steps to that end. Failure to come up to these expectations may arouse suspicions that he is malingering and thus tend to abolish exemption from usual role responsibilities.

In Western society the borderland between sickness and non-sickness is characteristically occupied by a variety of syndromes which may, without further discussion here, be termed psychiatric illnesses. Where people draw the dividing-line between sick and non-sick depends on the extent to which they feel that the particular actors concerned can be held responsible or called to account for their feelings or behaviour. Actors labelled as 'neurotics' may well be regarded as ineligible for the sick role if people think that they are, or ought to be, able to control their feelings and behaviour. In other cases it is the appropriateness of the sick role rather than the actors' eligibility for it which is questioned. Thus it is often thought more suitable for those suffering from what are generally described as mental or nervous complaints to make an effort of will to change their outlook or circumstances, perhaps with the help of priests or other non-medical advisers, than to seek treatment from doctors. Whether this is so or not often depends, among other things, on the nature of the symptoms and signs presented by the sufferer. In certain instances, however, failure to fulfil the requirements of the sick role may in itself be seen by those concerned as the most significant indication of illness. For example, the schizophrenic may not believe that he is ill and thus may fail to see the necessity of taking any steps to get well; and a person suffering from a severe depressive illness, far from wanting to get well, may only wish to die. In such cases any failure to fulfil all the expectations involved in the sick role may be overshadowed in people's minds by what is regarded as the individual's lack of responsibility for such failure.

In what follows, some of the problems involved in examining the part played by religious concepts in people's attitudes towards mental illness are discussed in relation to the structure of a particular local community comprising the people who live in one small parish in a rural area in South Wales. It seems clear that, although organized religion plays a relatively small part in the life of the community, ideas about behaviour spring from an outlook of a religious kind which is basically Christian in character. This outlook permeates all sections of the parish population, but there appear to be differences between certain social categories in the extent to which emphasis is placed on personal accountability in the evaluation of feelings and behaviour.

SOCIAL STRUCTURE

The parish consists of about 1,500 acres of land with a population of about 120 people. Most of the houses are scattered quite widely over the area of the parish, with three clusters, each of about half a dozen dwellings, at road junctions. There is no nucleated village in the sense of a compact grouping of church, farmsteads, houses and cottages. The seventeenth and eighteenth centuries saw the disappearance of freeholders from the parish. From about 1740 until 1961 almost the whole parish formed a major part of a large landed estate owned by absentee landlords. For more than two hundred years the agent or steward of the estate therefore assumed great importance in the parish. Many holders of the office lived in the parish but latterly the agent lived elsewhere and ran the affairs of the estate from an office in a large town less than twenty miles away.

At the census of 1851 the population of the parish was 220. Apart from the agent of the estate, the most prominent residents were: the rector, a clergyman of what was then the Established Church of England in Wales; the schoolmaster; and about a dozen tenant farmers. The population also included a number of skilled craftsmen, such as a blacksmith, wheelwright, tailor, and shoemaker. There were two small shops or general stores in the parish and one inn or public house. The remainder of the working population consisted of manual labourers of various kinds, most of them agricultural workers and farmers' servants. In 1851 there were about 50 children in the National School and, as far as one can tell, most of the people who then lived in the parish also earned their livings largely within its boundaries.

Fifty years later, in 1901, the population had fallen to 115. This was the result of three main factors; the agricultural depression of the 1880s; the rapid growth of urban areas and the coal industry, which combined with the low standards of rural housing to produce wholesale migration of farm workers and their families to the towns; greatly improved communications, including in 1875 the coming of the railway to within a mile of the parish boundary.

Since 1901 the size of the population has remained about the same. But in other ways the changes have been even greater than in the preceding fifty years. In 1951 there was no longer a resident parish priest of what had, in 1920, become the disestablished Church in Wales, a separate province of the Anglican communion. The school had been closed for more than ten years and it was more than thirty years since there had been a shop or pub in the parish. It was to neighbouring villages a mile or two away that children went to school and people went to shop, meet friends, play darts, and drink beer. By 1962 only three out of the thirty-seven households in the parish were without some form of motor transport. This makes up for the fact that the railway closed many years ago and that the nearest available public transport is provided by buses on the main road which runs at least a mile from most houses in the parish.

Between 1945 and 1961 the freeholds of six houses were sold by the estate to 'newcomers' who either worked in urban areas less than twenty miles away or had retired from work in those areas to a place in the country. At the same time four houses were built in the parish by the local authority for renting to agricultural workers; but only one of the four has ever been occupied by such a tenant. In fact the most striking recent change in the parish is that only twelve of the thirty-seven households include individuals earning their living from work carried on within its boundaries. Two of these households involve agricultural labourers. The remainder are the households of farmers.

Until 1961 all the farmers in the parish, and all the other householders apart from 'newcomers' and local authority tenants, were tenants of the estate. In that year the freeholds of the twenty-seven holdings of the estate were sold to a consortium of the tenants and almost overnight a community which had for two centuries been one mainly of tenants became one mainly of owner-occupiers.

Later in this paper I propose to discuss some of the findings of a study carried out in the parish and designed to explore the relation between symptom prevalence and attitudes to symptoms. It formed the pilot survey for a larger-scale study pursued in the local rural area as a whole. The most important general hypothesis underlying these studies is that differences in symptom prevalence and in attitudes to symptoms would be found to exist in different sections of the local population. Fieldwork carried out in the area had already shown that a number of social groupings could be identified, each of which clearly represented local sub-cultures. Analysis of social roles filled by members of each grouping indicated a number of simple variables which were used as the principal items of information obtained for every individual in a private census of every household in the area. Census data then formed the basis for dividing the whole population, comprising some 13,000 people, into a number of categories or groupings for use in the sample surveys. Some aspects of the theoretical background of this operation have been discussed elsewhere (Loudon, 1961).

It would be idle to pretend that the procedure used for subdividing a population of 13,000 is likely to provide a very sensitive analysis of the social alignments among the 120 people who live in the parish. At the same time, it is quite legitimate shorthand to say that virtually everyone in the parish is a member of one or other of three main sections, each of which consists of people who have in common a number of objectively defined social characteristics and who show by their behaviour that they see themselves as being of roughly the same perceived social status. These three sections I shall call middle class, working class, and farmers.

There are 7 middle-class households in the parish with a total of 24 occupants. No adult members of these households were born or brought up in the parish; only two, both members of the same household, were born within about ten miles of the parish; and none has lived in the parish for more than fifteen years. There are no effective ties of kinship between any members of these households and other households in the parish; but in three cases there are such ties with other households in the vicinity. The occupations represented in these households, other, of course, than that of housewife, can all be classified as professional, executive, or managerial, and all adults had some form of secondary education, with in many cases some form of higher education.

The 17 working-class households include 56 individuals. The occupations represented can all be classified as manual, with the single exception of one clerical officer in local government. Only six adults had any education after the minimum school-leaving age. Only three households are without an adult member born and brought up either in the parish or in the locality; the same three are the only examples of working-class households without effective kin ties in the locality. Eleven households have close ties of kinship with not less than two other working-class households in the parish. Two households also have effective kin ties with farmer households in the parish.

There are 13 farmer households in the parish with a total of 40 occupants. Only two adults among them are not either farmers or farmers' wives; one farmer has a son who works as a motor mechanic; another has a daughter who is a shorthand-typist. Only a few of the younger men and women in this section had any kind of secondary education. With one exception, all farmer households have effective kin ties with other farmers in the parish and in the locality; two, as already indicated, also have kin ties with working-class households in the parish. All farmer households have at least one adult member born and brought up in the locality and only two are without an adult member born and brought up in the parish.

The part of South Wales in which the parish is situated is a particularly English area of a county which has become steadily more Anglicized over the past hundred years or more with the development of major industries. Nevertheless most of the people describe themselves as Welsh and feel themselves to be Welsh in such contexts as International Rugby Football, although very few of them speak more than a few words of the Welsh language and more than half the surnames represented in the parish are non-Welsh in origin; and both of the two principal religious denominations with which parishioners are involved are nominally Welsh in character and background.

RELIGIOUS ORGANIZATION

Organized religion in the parish centres upon the parish church, a small and pleasant building dating mainly from the fourteenth century. But organized religion among parish people involves other places of worship outside the parish boundaries. The most significant of these is Zion, the Welsh Presbyterian (formerly Calvinistic Methodist) chapel, built in 1835 on the outskirts of a village about a mile away. About fifteen people in the parish go to church or chapel regularly, by which I mean not less often than once a month. Of these about ten go to the parish church and five go to Zion. Only for the parish church does this give any impression of the size of the congregation at the one service held there every Sunday morning; the average for the three years 1958, 1959, and 1960 was about seven. The chapel draws worshippers from a comparatively wide area and has an average congregation on Sunday mornings of about twenty people.

How far do attendances at religious services reflect membership of religious organizations? For the church one answer can be obtained by analysis of the Electoral Roll, which contains the names of all those in the parish who are eligible as electors for and members of the Parochial Church Council. The essential qualifications for inclusion are confirmed membership of the Anglican communion and being over the age of 21. The Electoral Roll is drawn up each year before the annual meeting of the vestry at Easter, and any necessary modifications are then made. Between 1952 and 1962 the number of electors resident in the parish varied between 24 and 32, with an average of 27. This number is roughly the same as the average number of Easter communicants, the most usual index of membership used by the Church. In addition, there were each year five or six individuals on the Roll who were not resident; these are mostly people previously resident who maintain some kind of connection with the church through relatives who still live in the parish. In the ten-year period, however, there was a considerable turnover in the membership of the Electoral Roll. Of the 26 resident electors in 1952, only 12 remained as such in 1962; of the other 14 individuals, 5 had by then died and 8 had moved out of the parish. The remaining individual, though continuing to reside in the parish, asked for her name to be removed from the Roll following divorce from her husband, principally because she is the daughter of one of the two churchwardens in whose household she and her two children live. By 1962, when there were 24 resident electors, 18 individuals had had their names added to the Roll; of these 11 were newcomers, 6 were residents who came of age, and one was a long-time resident accidentally omitted from the Roll for many years. Within the ten-year period, however, 5 of these additions to the Roll left the parish and one died.

Precisely comparable figures for Nonconformists in the parish are not obtainable. As far as Zion is concerned, the average number of communicants at the Chapel each year was 43. Of these an average of 6 individuals in each year were resident in the parish and aged over 21. No newcomers to the parish became communicants at Zion; 5 individuals remained communicants throughout the period; 2 died; and 2 came of age. Some comparison may, however, be made of the pattern of office-holding in Church and Chapel.

In the Church the only offices of any real significance are

those of minister and churchwarden. There are two church-wardens; one (the so-called people's warden) being elected by the Parochial Church Council, and one (the rector's warden) being appointed by the minister. Throughout the period under review the office of minister in charge of the parish was occupied by the same individual who was also the vicar of the neighbouring parish in which he lived. The people's warden also remained unchanged, the office being held by an elderly woman who succeeded her mother in the position about 20 years ago. The daughter of an agricultural labourer and the wife of a semi-skilled worker at a local quarry, she is also the organist, care-taker, and cleaner of the church, for which duties she is paid £10 a year. Four men held the office of rector's warden between 1952 and 1962; they were all 'newcomers' to the parish and all 'middle class' by occupation, education, and income. The holder of office in 1962 was a company director; of his three predecessors one died, one moved away from the parish, and one resigned. The other offices in the Church consist of sidesmen, whose principal duty is to take the collection during services; members of the Parochial Church Council; and the Council's secretary. Elections to these offices are held at the annual meeting of the vestry, which has been attended since 1952 by an average of five parishioners. The secretary of the Council throughout the period has been the rector's warden; the members of the Council, six in number, have throughout con-sisted of the sidesmen, the churchwardens, and two others. In at least one instance, an elected member of the Council did not know for over two years that he was an office-holder. In 1962 twelve offices (excluding the minister) were filled by six indivi-duals of whom three were 'middle class', two were 'working class', and one was a farmer's wife.

In the Chapel the office-holders take a very much more active part in day-to-day affairs than is the case in the Church, where decisions tend to be taken by the minister with the acquiescence of the churchwardens. In the Chapel there is one minister – who is also the 'pastor' of no less than three other chapels in the district – five elders, a secretary, financial secretary, supply secretary, Sunday-school secretary, missionary secretary, organ-ist, and caretaker. In 1962 these twelve offices (excluding the minister) were filled by eight individuals, six being farmers or farmer's wives, and two being 'working class'.

From these details it can be shown that in 1962, out of a parish population of 85 adults, only about 30 individuals took some active part in organized religion, including those who only did so on such special occasions as Christmas and Easter. But there were very few who took no part at all in any kind of public religious ceremony during the year; most people attended a baptism, a wedding, or a funeral. A number of people who go to church only on ceremonial occasions also generally make a point of attending the annual Harvest Thanksgiving service in the autumn, when the interior of the church is festooned with flowers, fruit, and vegetables. Harvest festival is the principal occasion – and the only regular occasion – when nominal non-conformists and those who are without denominational commitment may be expected to attend a religious service in the parish church. This is the case in all parishes in the area and tends to produce a certain amount of cautious thunder from the Anglican clergy about primitive pagan survivals.

RELIGIOUS AFFILIATIONS

All middle-class households in the parish have some kind of link with the Church, just as all farming households have similar links with the Chapel or with other Nonconformist denominations. Roughly half the working-class households have some kind of connection with the Church, and half with the Chapel. This pattern of allegiance is much the same in other parts of rural Wales. It seems probable that the extent to which members of the working class retain connections with the Church in an area where Nonconformity had great impact and remains influential may be related in part to the fact that in the not so distant past many of them depended for their livelihoods on the goodwill and approval of the Anglican clergy and middle-class Anglican employers. In the parish there is also a suggestion that the existence of Church charities may have been a deciding factor. One farmer remembers his grandfather trying to persuade a labourer's widow to attend the Chapel of which he was a leading supporter; she refused, saying: 'There's a shilling or two to be had for going to Church, but not one penny at the Chapel meeting'.

When forced to answer a question about their religious affiliations, most people in the parish manage to align themselves with one or other of a number of Christian denominations. For the minority who take an active part the question does not of course raise problems; most of the inactive majority have some residual allegiance to the denomination of their parents, or to that according to which they were baptized or married. As elsewhere, those who say they belong to no organized religious body generally say they are Anglican when, for example, they are admitted to hospital or join the Army. There is also a large minority who have multiple allegiances of varying intensity which do not necessarily make it difficult for them to align themselves when forced to do so. One man, for example, was baptized a Methodist, although the son of a Baptist mother and a father who was 'nothing'; he went to a Methodist Sunday School and later became a lukewarm Congregationalist when his mother died and he was 'adopted' by his father's sister, who had become a Congregationalist at her marriage. He himself subsequently married an Anglican in the parish church, since when he has been inside a church or chapel only for weddings and funerals. Nevertheless, he claims to be an Anglican 'because the wife is Church and that is where I'll be buried'. Such claims as this do not arouse any criticism from most people in the parish. Only the minister and some of the small core of active church members sometimes complain that, though everyone in the parish has the right to be baptized and buried by the church, none of those claiming to be Church people, on however slender a ground, ever do anything to help the church materially or financially. From what has been said it will be clear that any kind of denominational census of the population is of doubtful value because of differences in the nature and strength of religious affiliations; but the following table gives at least some outline of the principal religious divisions of households in the three sections of the parish population.

It may be noted that the single household which has links with a denomination other than Anglican or Nonconformist includes an elderly lapsed Roman Catholic.

Affiliation	Middle-Class Households	Farmer Households	Working-Class Households	Total
Anglican	4	–	4	8
Nonconformist	–	3	1	4
Predominantly Anglican plus Nonconformist links	3	7	6	16
Predominantly Anglican plus other links	–	–	1	1
Predominantly Nonconformist plus Anglican links	–	3	5	8
Total	7	13	17	37

From time to time marriages have been performed by the Anglican minister in the parish church when neither of the two individuals concerned was Anglican, though at least one of them has had some kind of residential qualification or other connection with the parish. Such practices are officially frowned on by the Church in Wales but the nature of the incumbent's freehold gives him considerable latitude to decide such matters for himself; it is undoubtedly much more difficult for the parson in a small rural parish to refuse marriage in the church in such cases than it is for ministers of large urban parishes. Among the people themselves there is now very little if any feeling expressed against mixed marriages between Anglicans and Nonconformists, even among the close kin of the bride and bridegroom, unless there are other reasons for disapproval of the match. Sometimes when there is felt to be a difference between the spouses, not only in religious affiliation but also in social status, objections by parents on the latter ground tend to be focused publicly on the former; in most cases, but by no means in all, those withholding approval in this way are Anglicans who consider that their child is making a hypogamous marriage. There is, however, very considerable reluctance among all members of Protestant religious bodies to approve of marriages with Roman Catholics. One informant, an Anglican farmer's wife discussing her son's future marriage, put it this way: 'I don't care who he marries as long as she's a nice girl. It doesn't matter to me whether she's Church or Chapel as long as she's a farmer's daughter and makes him a good wife. Mind you, there's a lot of riff-raff belong to the Church; I'd rather he married a Chapel girl of the right type, you know, even if it meant him going over to the Chapel himself, than one of them. As for marrying a Roman Catholic, I wouldn't have it; over my dead body.'

RELIGION AND BEHAVIOUR

In recent years a number of religious bodies have shown increased awareness of the field of mental health as one in which they feel their members have a particular obligation to take an active interest. A series of exhortations to this effect have been made at a national level by leaders of various denominations and a number of efforts have been made to establish the need for consultation between doctors and ministers in dealing with problems of mental illness. Nevertheless, most clergy in the rural area in which the parish is situated seem to feel inadequately equipped by training to deal with cases of mental illness among their parishioners or among members of their congregations. Some feel guilty or perplexed by their evident inability to deal with problems which they remain convinced are primarily spiritual matters involving loss of faith or loss of touch with God. Others appear to hold a more robust if somewhat Gadarene point of view, well expressed by one preacher at Harvest Festival, who stormed at the packed pews in front of him: 'You don't use your minds. You sit in front of the television set and your minds get flabby. That is why there are more and more people needing to be taken into institutions for mental defectives'. When faced with illness most ministers in the area, whether Anglican or Nonconformist, put forward the orthodox view that disease and death are not part of the divinely inspired order of things. Few of them seem to find it easy to discuss such matters informally outside the pulpit, partly because they believe that the basic Christian teaching which links disease with sin is misunderstood and rejected by the bulk of the population, and partly because of personal difficulties in reconciling the requirements of doctrine with pastoral experiences. One minister in the area spoke of 'the tensions which Holy Orders

bring with them, and particularly those which arise from the
necessity to be winning and tender towards individuals, and yet
resolute as guardians of the Word and Sacraments'. In two
instances where local clergy suffered from attacks of depressive
illness severe enough to require admission to hospital for
electro-convulsive therapy, the disorder was accompanied in
one case by expression of loss of faith in the goodness of God,
in the other of loss of belief in God's existence. Some of the
other ministers in the area who visited these men in hospital
said that moments of doubt occurred to all ministers but that
only in a man already ill for other reasons, such as physical
stress or fatigue or the financial and other anxieties of his
profession, would it be possible for these doubts to develop to
such an extent as to 'cause' depressive illness. One minister
said that in his view 'depression is a sickness of the mind which,
even in a man whose life is ordained to the service of God, can
flow over and cause a sickness of the soul which showed itself
by the denial of all that he had hitherto held to be true'.

In the ordinary course of events most people in the parish
do not talk much about religion. At a superficial level of discussion they tend to equate religious observance with religious
belief; this may be why members of both sexes expect women to
be more concerned than men with religious affairs, since women
are more frequent and regular attenders at church and chapel
services and are more insistent than men on the need for infant
baptism and religious instruction in schools, and on the importance of religious ceremonial at marriages and funerals. Irre-
spective, however, of whether or not they themselves take much
part in organized religious activities, people do not necessarily
seem to think that a man who only goes to church or chapel
on special occasions is therefore, and for that reason alone,
unlikely to hold perfectly orthodox Christian beliefs; nor do
they always feel that the assiduous church- or chapel-goer is
necessarily more 'religious' than those who hardly ever visit a
place of worship.

In so far as people in the parish use a series of dimensions in
characterizing each other's qualities and behaviour, the dimension represented by the word 'religious' is much less important
as implying particular kinds of belief than as indicating high

moral standards, honest dealings, and good neighbourliness based on Christian teachings. It is also said that a good test of the depth and sincerity of religious beliefs is provided by the way people react when suffering severe misfortunes. The wife of a man who, though a regular church-goer, is widely held to be an adulterer and petty thief, died suddenly at a comparatively early age. Conclusive evidence of the husband's hypocrisy was thought to have been provided by his effusive demonstration of grief before and during the funeral; people said that no man with real religious beliefs could have wept so openly, continuously, and noisily in the church and at the graveside after the way he had treated his wife for so many years. In other cases the stoicism under suffering of those who have declared themselves to be without religious beliefs is sometimes pointed to as showing that they were deceiving themselves. Without some kind of religious faith, people say, you can't get through times of real trouble. Others put it slightly differently, emphasizing the comfort religious practices bring without necessarily mentioning beliefs. One woman, a nominal Nonconformist who said she had little time or inclination for bothering about religion, was married to an openly sceptical man who nevertheless declared himself to be an Anglican; when her husband died the body was privately cremated and the ashes brought back to the parish for a funeral service in the church. Some weeks later, knowing that I had talked about religion with her husband, she referred to the decision to hold a religious ceremony, saying that it was comforting to find that friends and neighbours expected to be able to come to the funeral. A little later in the conversation she mentioned a cremation which she had once attended where the dead person was, as she described him 'a good man but an atheist or freethinker or some such – and most of his family the same'. She said that no religious service was held but a friend of the family 'read bits of poetry and then it was all over and it was so much worse than an ordinary funeral where everyone knows what to expect and what to do'. She indicated that she thought it was unnecessarily harrowing for people to be so rigid; she said, 'What is religion for if not to help people at such times?' Other informants have given examples of people who never went to church or showed much sign of religious belief who, when they suffered personal tragedies, talked repeatedly of the will of God. Similarly those who find themselves faced with the task of comforting the afflicted fall back on the same kind of pious formula, as a readily available and acceptable way of indicating appropriate sentiments without risking the display of disorderly emotion. No doubt in many cases such statements are also a kind of 'recognition of real ambiguities in experience rather than a pious aspiration towards resignation to the will of an ultimately benevolent personal God' (Lienhardt, 1961, p. 54).

It is often said that there is a close link between a people's predominant beliefs about the nature of human society and its place in the universe, and the moral standards they employ in social relations; that beliefs and ideas influence social life and social life influences beliefs and ideas. Examinations of the relation between these elements often boil down to a kind of 'facile interactionism' in which the view is put forward that 'beliefs and actions are distinct and separately identifiable social phenomena' (MacIntyre, 1962, p. 49). Nevertheless there are circumstances in which beliefs have of necessity to be considered apart from actions, as for example in differentiating between ceremonial and ritual; here the significance for social relations of a particular kind of behaviour depends upon the beliefs of the participants in the form of the standardized procedures having intrinsic validity or efficacy through the operation of a special mystical quality. In any society there are occasions when some of those present, because they hold such beliefs, see themselves as taking part in a rite, whereas others who do not share these beliefs are attending what is for them no more than a ceremony.

Unless it is thought to indicate mental illness, total discrepancy between the stated beliefs of an individual and his behaviour may suggest insincerity or, at best, self-deception; but less flagrant discrepancies between what people do and what they say they believe serve to remind us of the fact that 'actions, as much as utterances, belong to the realm of statements, concepts and beliefs'. Inconsistencies emphasize the relation between beliefs and actions as one which 'is not contingent but logical. . . . It is because actions express beliefs, because actions are a vehicle for (people's) beliefs, that they can be described as consistent or inconsistent with beliefs expressed in avowals' (MacIntyre, 1962, p. 52). Apparent inconsistencies are an important element in the system of religious beliefs found in the parish. Although organized religion does not play a large part in the life of the inhabitants, it will be clear that most of them seem to feel the need to recognize a religious component in certain social situations. This is true, not only for those who are lukewarm in their acceptance of Christian theology, but also for those who, while denying that they are atheists, are more or less open sceptics at least as far as utterances are concerned. One working-class ex-serviceman, for example, does not attempt to conceal his impatience with most aspects of formal religion and speaks ironically of the God whose existence he doubts as 'that old bugger up top'; but he always makes a point of solemnly observing Remembrance Day and says it is wrong for small children not to be taught to say their prayers. For him, as for most of his fellow-parishioners, social order is seen, albeit vaguely, as a matter fundamentally of religious order. To describe a man as an atheist is to use a term of opprobrium, for atheism is understood to mean much more than a denial of the existence of God; it is also taken to imply a denial that Christ ever existed, together with active opposition to the moral principles enunciated in the New Testament. Though the former implication is seen as a ludicrous flight in the face of evidence, the latter is liable to be considered potentially subversive and dangerous. Everybody in the parish with whom I have pressed the point falls back on some interpretation, however idiosyncratic, of Christian teaching as the distant and final authority for right behaviour; but very few think that God acts in any way as a direct agent of retribution for those in breach of moral regulations. Most see the influence of religion as operating through men's consciences; but they tend to regard conscience as a faculty almost of the same kind as memory or reason, something which, however it is played upon by experiences and circumstances, is intrinsic to all human beings, and is the same for everyone. There are occasions when conscience, like other faculties, is spoken of as something in which a few people may possibly be deficient or which in rare circumstances may become diseased. But, in general, behaviour which is considered bad is seen as the result of an individual failing to attend to the promptings of his conscience; and whether an individual does so or not is thought to be a matter of volition.

On the face of it, therefore, in so far as the parish is representative of contemporary British society, there seems little justification for religious leaders saying that people are less influenced by Christian ethics today than they were in the past. What I have called the concept of accountability is in effect the operation of notions of guilt and responsibility, of society and its members being answerable for their behaviour, and of some kinds of misfortunes being the result of failures to observe the injunctions of symbolic guardians of moral order. I now propose to discuss the importance of these notions for the identification of mental illness.

CONCEPTS OF MENTAL DISORDER

The kind of image which leaps to the mind of most people in the parish when mental illness is mentioned is fairly easy to determine from remarks made about acquaintances who have been admitted to mental hospitals. Surprise is frequently shown at the absence from individual cases of one or more of a number of factors which are thought to be characteristic of it, for mental disorder is thought of as a single phenomenon, as a serious, relatively incurable state, characterized by wild, unpredictable, and often dangerous behaviour, usually accompanied by some intellectual impairment; in other words, concepts of mental illness are narrowly confined in practice to certain aspects of psychosis. On the other hand, people in the parish think of 'nervous' illness as a separate entity, not only more transient and much less severe than mental illness, but quite different from it qualitatively. Many regard the nerves as something analogous with, but physically separate from, the brain and the rest of the body, and, most importantly, as something whose functioning can and should be controlled by the will.

Many of the difficulties involved in attempting to explore concepts of mental disorder are, of course, semasiological. A simple and obvious example is provided by the word 'mad', which may either describe someone who is insane, or someone who is angry, or someone who is of a scatter-brained and impetuous nature. People described as 'mental', on the other hand, are usually those thought to show signs of intellectual defect, whether congenital or acquired; thus the word may be used to describe an educationally subnormal child or an old person suffering from mild senile dementia. Even if careful note is made of the context, problems of interpretation may arise, as the following example shows. A young unmarried farmer was brought before the local magistrates accused of driving his motor-car in a wild and reckless manner; unknown to the authorities he had recently been discharged for the second time from a mental hospital, where he had been diagnosed as suffering from paranoid schizophrenia. His demeanour in court was unusually bizarre and disrespectful. I was interested to find that the local police chief, in private conversation, described him as being 'a bit on the mad side'; but when he went on to say that 'all these young farmers nowadays are a bit wild and cocky' it became clear that the word 'mad' did not mean that my informant had recognized the behaviour as any indication of psychopathology.

Perhaps the most flexible and illuminating of the many terms commonly used by people in the parish is the phrase 'not right'. Although essentially no more than a shortened version of 'not right in the head' or 'not in his right mind', it has a variety of shades of meaning. Sometimes it is employed euphemistically, in contexts where it is more tactful than an outright declaration that someone may be insane, or where such a declaration goes further towards burning the bridges of social relations than the speaker is willing to venture. The phrase is often used by people when they are discussing the apparently deranged behaviour of a close relative or friend, but are either reluctant to face the possible significance of what they have observed or unwilling to abandon the hope that the aberration may prove temporary. In such cases to say of someone that he is 'not right' suggests behaviour which is unusual in a relatively mild but rather ominous way.

When the speaker is less intimately involved the phrase may

be used in one of a number of other slightly different ways. For example, when the actions or demeanour of an individual are widely held to betoken mental illness, but remain unacknowledged as such by the individual's immediate relatives, it may be used by neighbours among themselves as a simple and unambiguous synonym for insanity. Again it may describe an individual who is predictably unpredictable, as in the case of a man who is well known to be subject to ungovernable outbursts of rage when drunk but who is otherwise seemingly perfectly normal; here the phrase implies a latent tendency rather than an actual state. But the most frequent usage is when people think it advisable, for the long-term maintenance of good relations with neighbours, to explain or excuse small acts of uncharacteristic bad behaviour; the phrase is then employed to absolve the actor from accountability for failures to fulfil expectations of friendliness or helpfulness.

In other circumstances, however, especially where face-to-face relationships are not involved, it is more usual to find examples of aberrant behaviour which are generally considered morally reprehensible even though they suggest the presence of mental disorder to what have been termed the 'ratifiers', that is to say, 'those who have the public mandate, in so far as one exists, to stamp' the mental patient as such (Goffman, 1957, p. 202). The existence of differences in the readiness with which the yardstick of accountability is applied to deviant behaviour is the subject of considerable contemporary public discussion, though the debate tends to condense round the supposed gap between the views of the general public on this matter and the opinions of such 'ratifiers' as the psychiatrists. In this essay I am concerned with contrasts of another kind.

THE PREVALENCE OF MENTAL DISORDER

National figures for the prevalence of certain mental disorders show that there are significant differences between, among others, the main socio-economic categories of the population. Most of the information available is based almost entirely on returns of cases which have declared themselves to hospital and other psychiatric services, and on surveys of those patients who

91

consult their family doctors. Among the factors relating to such differences, particularly to those concerning the less severe and most common psychiatric ailments, it seems reasonable to suppose that variations in attitudes to mental illness and medical care play an important part. Obvious steps towards investigating such variation in attitudes would involve looking at the different ways in which people evaluate certain kinds of feeling and action; examining the distinctions they make in identifying those items or combinations of items which they regard as indicating illness; and trying to establish the criteria by which they decide whether or not such illnesses are appropriate matters for medical advice or treatment. In order to test the feasibility of such an investigation on a larger scale, a survey was carried out specifically designed to explore some of these topics among the 85 adult members of the parish population; although the numbers involved were too small for any findings to have statistical significance, the results suggest that a similar investigation on a larger scale may prove fruitful. For present purposes discussion is confined to those aspects of the study concerning the prevalence of symptoms and the degree to which certain symptoms are considered to be evidence of illness.

The aim of the survey was to conduct structured interviews in their homes with all adult members of the parish population, using a questionnaire and a number of opinion and attitude scales. Of the 85 individuals available, 19 either refused to take part or 'lapsed' for other reasons. The proportion of 'lapses' for each of the three sections of the parish population was about the same. Out of 13 middle-class individuals, 11 were interviewed; out of 42 working-class, 32 were interviewed; and out of 30 members of farming households, 23 were interviewed. There were thus 66 individuals for whom interview schedules were completed, consisting of 32 men and 34 women with mean ages of 50 and 47 years respectively. In the first part of the interview, each individual was asked to indicate whether he or she suffered from any of about 100 symptoms, half of which may be described as predominantly 'physical' in character, half as predominantly 'psychological'. For each symptom where the answer was in the affirmative the respondent was asked, among other things, to say whether medical or other advice had been sought. In the second part of the interview respondents were presented with a sequence of about a dozen 'profiles' of people suffering from various symptoms, half of which again were physical and half psychological. For each profile questions were asked aimed at discovering the extent to which respondents thought that the sufferer should be held accountable for his feelings and behaviour, and the extent to which they felt the symptoms described were appropriate matters for medical treatment or advice.

The results appear to indicate that there are certain differences both between male and female respondents and between members of the three sections of the parish population. For example, both men and women in the working class reported an appreciably larger mean number of physical symptoms than men and women members of farming households; the latter in turn reported a larger number of physical symptoms than middle-class men and women. A similar gradient was found in the declaration of psychological symptoms among male respondents; those in the middle class reported the smallest number of such symptoms and those in the working class the largest number. Among women, however, while members of the middle class declared the smallest number of psychological symptoms, it was the women-folk in farming households who reported the largest number; furthermore, among members of both sexes in all three sections, it was only for women in the farming section that the mean number of psychological symptoms was greater than that of physical symptoms.

From the results of those parts of the inquiry which attempted to measure differences in ideas about accountability for symptoms it is clear that members of both sexes in all three sections of the population had a tendency to regard people suffering from physical symptoms as more deserving of sympathy than those with psychological symptoms, as less expected to be able to control their feelings and behaviour, and as in general better fulfilling the expectations of the sick role. This tendency was most marked among male middle-class respondents, who showed the greatest readiness to require people with psychological symptoms to 'pull themselves together' and to declare it relatively less appropriate for sufferers from such symptoms to consult doctors.

Some social scientists become impatient with studies of small communities because of the difficulty of testing statistically any conclusions based on them. As far as the inquiry reported here is concerned, it seems possible that a further study on a larger scale, carried out on a stratified random sample of the inhabitants of the whole rural area, may confirm such apparent differences as were found in the parish between sections of the population both in the mean number of symptoms reported by respondents and in the ways in which they evaluate certain kinds of feeling and action. A further dimension of great importance will be added when records are available regarding the frequency with which members of the population sample seek medical advice and the nature of the complaints for which it is sought. It may then be possible to compare sections both in relation to expectations of accountability for symptoms and in relation to the ways, and the extent to which, psychopathology presents itself to individuals and is presented by them to doctors.

It is not enough, however, simply to show that certain special differences appear to exist between what may be called local sub-cultures. The identification of sub-cultures in itself involves the building of models, each of which is composed of more or less differing elements requiring detailed examination if we are to seek for correlates of variations between models. The models themselves I have here called middle-class, working-class, and farming sections of the population. Some of the elements of which they are composed are indicated by the titles given to them, titles which were intended to reflect parishioners' own usage and the varying emphasis they place on such elements as social status, ideology, and occupation; others have already been mentioned very briefly in an earlier part of this essay, including, for example, level of formal educational attainment and extent of local orientation and attachment. Variations in religious alignments and commitment have been examined in some detail; such inclination towards one or other of the main religious denominations as may be found in the three sections seem much less important than the contrast for the population as a whole between the part played by organized religion and the influence on moral judgements of ideas of a religious kind. In so far as moral judgements are involved in the evaluation of unusual behaviour, any theory put forward to explain differences between sections in such evaluation must therefore relate them to other structural elements. Elsewhere I have suggested that one important dimension in this respect is that of degree of homogeneity (Loudon, 1961, p. 349). Among the farmers and among most of the working class in the parish, social networks are remarkably close-knit; most members of these two sections who remain there are those who lack strong aspirations towards social or physical mobility; role-relationships are long standing, tend to be multiple with the same people and are mediated by direct face-to-face interaction. While these characteristics might be expected to produce a situation where little variation in individual behaviour would be sanctioned, it seems clear that judgements as to whether role-performances are unusual or not tends to be in terms of flexible local norms which are adaptable to particular circumstances. Among middle-class people, however, evaluation of behaviour tends to be in terms of national norms which emphasize the expected capacity of the individual to control himself, his destiny, and his environment. Admittedly such a description contains an element of caricature; but some aspects of it may be linked to the fact that most of the middle class in the parish are people without long-standing local attachments who have deliberately moved into the area as part of a process of upward social mobility or as a means of maintaining their own perceived social position in the relative isolation of a small rural community.

REFERENCES

BEIDELMAN, T. O. 1963. Witchcraft in Ukaguru. In J. Middleton & E. H. Winter. (eds.), *Witchcraft and Sorcery in East Africa*. London: Routledge & Kegan Paul.

EVANS-PRITCHARD, E. E. 1937. *Witchcraft, Oracles and Magic among the Azande*. Oxford: Clarendon Press.

—— 1956. *Nuer Religion*. Oxford: Clarendon Press.

FIRTH, R. 1959. Problem and Assumption in an Anthropological Study of Religion. *Journal of the Royal Anthropological Institute* **89**: 129-147.

GELLNER, E. 1962. Concepts and Society. *Transactions of the Fifth World Congress of Sociology* 1: 153-183.

GOFFMAN, E. 1957. On some convergences of sociology and psychiatry: a sociologist's view. *Psychiatry* 20: 201-203.

GOODY, J. 1962. *Death, Property, and the Ancestors.* Stanford: Stanford University Press; London: Tavistock Publications.

LIENHARDT, G. 1961. *Divinity and Experience: the Religion of the Dinka.* Oxford: Clarendon Press.

LOUDON, J. B. 1961. Kinship and Crisis in South Wales. *British Journal of Sociology* 12: 333-350.

MACINTYRE, A. 1962. A mistake about causality in social science. In P. Laslett & W. G. Runciman (eds.), *Philosophy, Politics and Society.* Oxford: Blackwell.

PARSONS, T. 1951. *The Social System.* Glencoe, Ill.: The Free Press; London: Tavistock-Routledge.

Adrian C. Mayer

The Significance of Quasi-Groups in the Study of Complex Societies

Two concepts of major importance for social anthropologists are those of group and association. Both have been defined in a number of ways. Even in the most inclusive view, however, both bodies are held to consist of a number of members with some form of expected interaction, if not rights and obligations, towards one another. Both the association and the group show an 'even spread' of the membership criteria on which this inter-action is based, whether these are highly informal or whether they produce a corporate body. Much fruitful work has been carried out with the aid of these concepts. Nevertheless, they are inadequate for those situations involving another kind of collection of people, which may be termed the 'quasi-group'.

Quasi-groups can be divided into two types. The first can be termed that of the classificatory quasi-group. Here, the classification may be made in terms of the common interests which lie beneath what could also be called a 'potential group'. Ginsberg, for example, defines quasi-groups as entities without a 'recogniz-able structure, but whose members have certain interests or modes of behaviour in common which may at any time lead them to form themselves into definite groups'.[1] The classification may also be made by an individual in terms of his perceived status *vis-à-vis* others, as Barnes shows in his analysis of class mentioned below. I do not propose to deal with this type of quasi-group. Rather, I shall confine myself to quasi-groups of the second type. These possess a degree of organization, but are nevertheless not groups. They can be called interactive quasi-groups, for they are based on an interacting set of people.

These quasi-groups differ fundamentally from the group and the association. First, they are ego-centred, in the sense of depending for their very existence on a specific person as a central organizing focus; this is unlike a group, in which organization may be diffuse. Second, the actions of any member are relevant only in so far as they are interactions between him and ego or ego's intermediary. The membership criteria do not include interaction with other quasi-group members in general.

The interactions of this type of quasi-group occur in an action-set[2] or rather in a series of action-sets. I wish to examine the properties of the action-set by studying it in operation. This I shall do from data gathered in India. But first I must show what is meant by 'set' and how it is related to social network.

NETWORK AND SET

Sets are embedded in the matrices of social links contained in social fields, which have also been called networks. Recent use of the terms 'set' and 'network' has been somewhat confusing, and I will therefore try to clarify the distinction between them.

The term network was used by Radcliffe-Brown (1952, p. 190) when he characterized social structure as being a 'network of actually existing social relations' and maintained that this structure should be the object of the anthropologist's investigation. The relations making up the structure were maintained by a convergence of interests, or at least a 'limitation of conflicts that might arise from divergence of interests' (ibid., p. 199). In some cases, the structure could be defined by a single criterion, as for instance in an Australian tribe, where 'the whole social structure is based on a network of such relations of person to person, established through genealogical connections' (ibid., p. 191).

As Firth (1954, p. 4) points out, Radcliffe-Brown used network to express impressionistically 'what he felt by describing metaphorically what he saw' and it was left to Barnes to give the term a more precise definition.

Barnes saw a network as a social field made up of relations between people. These relations were defined by criteria underlying the field – in the case he cites, for instance, these were criteria of neighbourhood and friendship which might in turn subsume kinship and economic connections. The network was 'unbounded' (at least, by the local boundary of the parish studied)[3] and was without leadership or a coordinating organization. Any person had relations with a number of other people, who in turn were linked to further people.[4] The links might cluster in some parts of the network; but if the people concerned formed a group, their group linkages would exist apart from the network, since an extra criterion would have been added to the linkages defining the network.

The definition of network formed the first step in Barnes's analysis. The second was the identification of sets of people on the basis of linkages provided by the network. The set was different in form from the network. For it was centred on a single person (ego), and consisted of the people classified by him according to a certain criterion. These people thus formed only part of the network – that part which ego recognized as being contained in the set. Barnes's purpose was to use the network-set concept to analyse social class. For him, classes consisted of those people whom an ego identified, through his linkages with them, as comprising sets with statuses above, equal to, or below him. The set did not form a group; nor was ego its leader. But it was at that moment a bounded entity. Moreover, the connections which ego had with the various people he identified in the class context were along 'paths' which might consist of more than one link. It should be noted that these sets lacked any purposive content, and can therefore be categorized as classificatory sets. Here, they differ from the interactive set of the type previously discussed by Chapple and Coon (1947, p. 283), with which I shall be concerned in this paper. Nevertheless, both types of set are similar in that they are ego-centred and may contain intermediaries between ego (the originator) and the terminal individuals.

The aspect of Barnes's analysis which has received most attention is his view of the network. Firth admits that the image it presents may be useful and vivid, and Nadel refers to it in his discussion of network. But neither writer considers the part played by the set in Barnes's scheme. For instance, Firth (1954, p. 4) sees Barnes's use of the network as 'a metaphor convenient to describe the personal sets of relationships which characterize the particular structure of a Norwegian fishing community'. I would rather suggest that Barnes conceives of the network as important in so far as it is a *basis* for sets rather than as a means of describing them, and that the two are distinct.

In her study of urban families, Bott uses the term to cover both of Barnes's concepts. On the one hand, a family maintains relationships of friendship, kinship, and neighbourhood with a certain number of other families; these constitute the family's network. On the other hand, each of the other families has its relations with yet other families, many of which are not connected to the initial family at all. Viewed, therefore, from the central family, there is a finite number of relations based on its own interaction, beyond which stretch further links (unbounded from this central family's viewpoint) which have nothing to do with it. Both the bounded and the 'unbounded' entities are included under the rubric network by Bott (1957, p. 58), though it would have been clearer to call the former a set. The articulation between the set of an ego (individual or family) and the network (or social field) which stretches away on all sides is provided by the fact that the 'lateral' links between units other than ego in the set are at the same time elements in other sets centred on these units. Nevertheless, at any given time the component units of a set have a known boundary; it is not one of group membership, as I have pointed out, but of their common connection to the central ego. It is this common link which enables Bott to treat her networks as unit entities which can be analysed and compared.

A reason for Bott's lack of distinction between network and set may well be provided by an ambiguity in Barnes's article itself. On the one hand, Barnes uses the term 'set' in his definition of network, saying

'. . . I find it convenient to talk of a social field of this kind as a *network*. The image I have is of a *set*[5] of points some of which are joined by lines. The points of the image are people, or sometimes groups, and the lines indicate which people interact with each other. . . . A network of this kind has no external boundary' (Barnes, 1954, p. 43, second italics mine).

Here, set is being used in an indefinite way, to denote the links of a network in the metaphorical way noted by Firth. On the other hand, Barnes uses the term in a different way when he talks of an individual 'generating his set of cognatic kin' and later says '. . . Thus for every individual A the whole of the network, *or at least that part of it of which he is aware*, is divided into three areas or sets of points' (Barnes, 1954, p. 46, my italics). Here, the set is bounded by ego's vision, and is centred on ego. This, I would maintain, is the more significant use of the word as far as analysis is concerned. But the fact that it is used differently in the two passages may have confused the distinction between the bounded and 'unbounded' entities.

Later writers have followed Bott rather than Barnes in their terminology. Thus, Epstein defines network with reference to a particular individual and the linkages he has with others, and goes on to make a distinction between different parts of this network according to the amount of interaction. Here, network is used in Barnes's sense of the set[6]. Again, Lancaster (1961, p. 326) briefly discusses network mainly in Bott's 'unbounded' sense of the word which, she notes, 'tends to interpret "network" in the Barnes manner'. After stressing the unsatisfactory analytical nature of such 'unbounded' entities, she advocates the use of a delimited unit 'such as the total set of Ego's recognized kin' and says that such a unit would be more suited to comparative analysis. This is, in fact, what I believe Barnes to have concluded; but it is not possible to know whether Lancaster was referring to his article here, since Barnes's use of set is not mentioned. Finally, I myself (Mayer, 1962, p. 275) have also referred to networks both as 'unbounded' as well as defined at a particular time (i.e. bounded); the latter I would now call sets.

It should be noted that Nadel also uses the term network, though in a rather different way. For he equates it to system, since he says that it is through 'abstracting from the concrete population and its behaviour the pattern or network (or "system") of relationships' (Nadel, 1957, p. 12) existing between role-playing actors that social structure is arrived at. Nadel notes that Barnes has used the term in a different sense but, though he recognizes the existence of 'open networks', he places his main emphasis on the systematic nature of the linkages between actors which form a network. The analysis of

Adrian C. Mayer

these kinds of linkages is crucial for Nadel in his building up of social structure on a basis of roles. For it is the interlocking of relationships – through the dichotomization of roles – which brings about an expansion of the areas of relationships into networks. These can be of an open-ended kind, similar to the fields envisaged by Barnes; or they can be into bounded sub-groups, whose systematic interrelation makes up the social structure. Nadel stresses that both kinds of network exist in a society, but he is more interested in the latter and therefore devotes little attention to the open-ended network.

To sum up: there has been an attempt by social anthropologists to put forward two concepts for dealing with social situations in which collections of people are found that do not form groups. One is the 'unbounded' network of relationships between pairs of people, making up a field of activity. The other is the finite set of linkages initiated by an ego, which forms part of such a network.[7] Despite some ambiguity over terminology, these two concepts are distinguished by both Barnes and Bott and by others. We can further distinguish between the classificatory set discussed by Barnes, and Bott's set (i.e. the 'network' of her analysis) which is based on interaction around an ego. The latter is made up of people brought into contact in a variety of situations and over a period of time. It is the sum, as it were, of the people involved in a series of purposive action-sets in specific contexts. To find out more about it, therefore, one must first inquire into the characteristics of the action-set. This I will do now, using my own material on political processes in India.

THE DEWAS ELECTORAL SITUATION

My data come from the Dewas District of Madhya Pradesh State in India.[8] The District has a population of 446,901 (1961) and is situated some 75 miles west of the State's capital of Bhopal, and 20 miles north-east of the industrial town of Indore. Part of it is prosperous farming country, in which cotton and wheat are major cash crops. Here is situated Dewas town, the District headquarters and only sizeable urban centre, with a population of 34,577 in 1961.

Until 1948, Dewas town was divided into halves, which were

102

the capitals of the States of Dewas Senior and Dewas Junior. The town was politically united after the Princely States were merged into the Indian Union in that year, and a single Municipality was constituted. The Municipal Council has a degree of autonomy in civic affairs, and is elected by universal suffrage. There have been three elections, and I wish to focus my attention on the last one, which took place in April 1961.

I have already given a general description of this event elsewhere (Mayer, 1963). There, I considered the types of workers active in the campaign, and the bases on which they and their candidates solicited and attracted votes. The various political parties each had a core of full-time election 'workers' (the English word being used). These primary workers helped with the organization of the campaign – by arranging meetings, etc., and helping to recruit secondary workers. The latter were people who would at least commit themselves to the support of a party (by contrast to a large part of the electorate) and who would perhaps join in canvassing parties and undertake to get the vote out in their localities. There were about 250 primary workers of all parties in the town's 14 wards, and perhaps between two and three times as many secondary workers, out of a total electorate of 16,332.

These workers acted as links between the candidate and the electorate. Sometimes they did this for the advantages they calculated would accrue to them if the candidate were elected; sometimes they were acting because of party loyalty and friendships formed over the years without any thoughts of gain from the election itself; and at yet other times they were discharging specific obligations contracted at earlier times. In the same way, there was an attempt to reach voters on the basis of a past or future benefit. As one shrewd observer told me, 'Every man will bleed; it is a question of knowing which is the vein to open so that he will bleed most.' In consequence, a great deal of the electioneering was carried out by workers, who sought to influence those with whom they had some appropriate relationship. Besides this, the candidate himself canvassed voters, often as a formal duty towards those who wished to have been asked for their vote. Both the general ideological and the local urban policies of the parties, as

Adrian C. Mayer

expressed in public meetings, were also deemed to have played some part in influencing voters. I am less interested in these latter aspects than in the pattern of interpersonal contacts through which votes were said to have been recruited; for it is from these that we can abstract the action-set. To show this I will present the detailed situation in one candidate's campaign.

The ward in which this candidate fought provided one of the key contests of the election. In the previous election, the seat had been won by the Congress party in a triangular contest with the Praja Socialists (PSP) and an Independent. Sixty per cent of the 852 electors had voted, and the Congress (with 210 votes) had just beaten the Independent (205 votes), though the 90 votes gathered by the PSP meant that victory was gained on a minority vote. In the succeeding term of the Municipality, the victor was said to have paid little attention to the repair of his political fences in the ward. He lived in another part of the town, and was a busy professional man. The Independent loser, on the other hand, was a resident of the ward. Over the years, he had built up strong support, partly through people's discontent with the sitting Councillor, and partly through the public and private work which he was sometimes able to do through intercession with officials and so forth.

At the 1961 election, then, the Independent stood again. This time he was an official Jan Sangh candidate. He himself did not appear to be an active party member, but received whatever support the rather sketchy Jan Sangh election organization was able to give him. He was opposed on Congress's behalf by another resident of the ward; this was a man who had recently retired from a senior government post, and who had previously held important appointments in the service of Dewas Senior, to which this part of the town had belonged. The candidate had not been a member of Congress before his retirement, and he too, therefore, was not part of the inner party organization; nevertheless, the support he received from Congress party leaders was considerably greater than that given to the Jan Sangh candidate. By contrast with his opponent, the Congress candidate had not built up any sort of ward support before being nominated, and had to start mobilizing followers there and then. The third candidate, representing the PSP, was a resident of the ward, but had little influence and received minimal support from PSP party leaders. The main contest was therefore between Congress and Jan Sangh.

Physically, economically, and socially, the ward is hetero-geneous. Situated at the north-eastern end of the town, a large part of its people live in mud houses built along earthen streets in the same style as in the surrounding villages. Other people live in houses similar to those of wealthier villagers, with inside courtyards formed by house and cattle byres; and yet others reside in urban-style houses surrounded by gardens. Beyond them lie barracks housing a detachment of the State's Special Armed Police, many of whom are eligible to vote. Within the ward, there is no meeting square and few stores exist. People gather mainly within each street, at informal sitting-places under a tree or on the porch of a temple or teashop. This has an obvious effect on the kind of election campaign that can be organized and strengthens the tendency to stress individual contacts, rather than to rely on public meetings.

A survey shows the main occupations of the population to be as set out in *Table 1*.

TABLE 1*

Occupation	%
Manual labour	38·2
Government officials	15·9
Farming and dairying	14·7
Pension	6·5
Construction: artisan and contractor	5·3
Commerce and hotel-keeping	5·3
Services: legal, domestic, medical, etc.	4·7
Other	9·4
Total	100·0

* These figures are compiled from a 20 per cent sample made on the basis of the 1957 voters' list: I doubt whether there have been great changes since then. The information was gathered from knowledgeable residents, rather than from a door-to-door inquiry, but is probably none the less accurate for that. The categories are those of the Dewas Census; where a woman's name appeared on the sample, her husband's occupation was taken.

As might be expected, occupations are to some extent

correlated with the main castes represented in the ward. The
same survey shows these to be as set out in *Table 2*.

TABLE 2

Caste	%
Goali	17·1
Bagri	17·1
Lunia	10·0
Balai	9·4
Rajput	8·2
Northern (Rangre) Brahman	8·2
Maratha	6·5
Maharashtrian Brahman	5·9
Other	17·6
Total	100·0

The Brahmans and Marathas are mainly in government
service, and many of the Rajputs farm land in the countryside
beyond the ward boundaries. In this, they have Goali and
Bagri farm labour; there are also a few Bagri policemen and
government messengers, and a number of Goali dairymen. For
the rest, the men of these castes are manual labourers, as are
the Balais and Lunias – the latter specializing in the building
trade. Hierarchically, below the Brahmans come Marathas and
Rajputs, and Goali, Lunia and Bagri, and Balai follow.

It is clear that a candidate cannot be elected on the support
of a single caste, or of a single occupational interest. Hence,
pressure has to be brought on various sections of the electorate.
This may be in terms of policy, or it may be through linkages
stretching from each candidate directly or through intermediaries to the voter. The pattern of the Congress candidate's
linkages, as they were described to me and as I observed them,
is given in the diagram.

I must stress that the diagram shows the links known to me.[9]
Further study would possibly have revealed others; but this
outline of the situation is, I believe, sufficient to indicate what
the full pattern would look like. Moreover, it is probable that, at
least where factions are involved, there are several further links
before the voter is reached; but I do not know enough about
these alignments to be able to show them diagrammatically.

THE PATTERN OF THE CONGRESS CANDIDATE'S LINKAGES

As I have pointed out, these are not the only contacts made by the candidate with the public; nor do they show all the reasons why people supported him. Some, for instance, may have done so because of his party's official policy; others may have voted for him because of the auspiciousness of his party's electoral symbol – the best example in the election of purely ideological support, which in other cases might underlie other reasons (e.g. support of a caste-mate is partly ideological and partly self-interested). But it is these links which are of interest, because I would maintain that they constitute an action-set in the context of this election. What are the characteristics of this action-set, and what is its relation to the underlying network?

One feature of this action-set is that a wide variety of bases for linkage are involved. Included as criteria are kinship, political party, religious sect, and so on. But the crucial point is that, whatever may be these 'outward' bases for the links which together make up the path from candidate to voter, the 'inward' content is always the same – namely political support of the candidate. Thus, action-sets of this kind are formed of links derived from many social fields; but because they are purposive creations by an ego, this purpose gives all the links a common feature, without which the action-set could not be classed under the quasi-group rubric. This results in an action-set whose structure may be similar to the classificatory set described by Barnes, but whose content is different. Rather, it is similar to the set envisaged by Chapple and Coon, at whose centre is an 'originator' of linkages.

A second feature of the action-set is that the links are sometimes, but not always, based on group membership. Many of the candidate's closest links were party-political ones, based on the primary group of active Congress workers which he joined upon his adoption as candidate. Other instances of primary group links are provided by membership of the same wrestling gymnasium, or of a group of religious worshippers.

Examples of links through secondary group membership would be those based on distant kinship relations,[10] and also, perhaps, membership of the same village or trade union – though these latter might be primary group links. Yet further from primary membership were the ties evoked through common caste. A crucial linkage, for example, was made between a Rajput Congress worker and Bagri voters. Bagris, officially a Backward Class, can produce 'historical' evidence which they believe gives them Rajput status. But this is not

108

generally accepted by the Rajputs of Malwa. Hence, when the Congress worker showed that he did not object to eating and drinking with Bagris in their homes, they were greatly attracted to the Congress candidate – particularly since the Rajput supporters of the Jan Sangh were strongly conservative over such matters. More than mere sentiment was involved; for it was said that the Rajput had told the Bagris that they could become members of the newly instituted Dewas branch of the Rajput Parishad, a social organization restricted to Rajputs.[11] I shall return later to this transactional element in linkages.

Some links are not based on group membership at all, of course. Examples would include the economic links of employer-employee, creditor-debtor, storekeeper-customer, etc. Again, people with a history of service to the Maharaja did not form part of any group. The fact that some links are based on group relations does not affect the form of the action-set. For such groups are not contained within the action-set, nor are their aims necessarily relevant to the purpose of the latter. The action-set is a different kind of entity from a group, though it may include group relations in its 'outward' content of links.

A third feature is that (as Barnes shows) the action-set contains paths of linkages, and is thus a combination of relationships linking people directly to ego, and of those linking people to intermediaries who are themselves in direct contact with ego. In this it differs from the units of Bott's analysis, which contained linkages between people who were all directly linked to ego; and one might find it useful to distinguish between simple and complex action-sets on this basis.

Fourth, the action-set is a bounded entity. It is not a group, however. For the basis for membership is specific to each linkage, and there are no rights or obligations relating all those involved; even the common act of voting for ego does not bring members into relation with each other.[12] Moreover, the action-set could not exist without the ego around whom it is formed. Yet, it is different in quality from a category. For members are aware that they form part of a population recruited for a particular common purpose, and they know that there are other linkages similar to theirs – though they may not be able to identify all the other people involved.

Adrian C. Mayer

Finally, the action-set is not a 'permanent' entity like the group. Although the 'outward' aspects are those of continuing role-relationships – e.g. those of caste, etc. – the 'inward' aspect is that of a linkage based on a specific purposive impulse stemming from ego. This action-set thus exists only at ego's election. Any action-set constructed for a future election might contain a majority of the same people. But many of the linkages would have to be re-made since, as I shall suggest later, they are based on specific transactions. To the extent that the same linkages remain in use in successive contexts of activity, a quasi-group is formed, as I shall discuss later.

THE ACTION-SET IN COMPARATIVE STUDY

A major feature of the action-set is that by contrast with the 'unbounded' network it is limited in its membership and can therefore be used in comparative analysis and in the study of social change. Let me give a few examples from the Dewas electoral situation I have described.

One could compare, for instance, the patterns of linkage in the action-sets of the three candidates in the ward. I did not study in such detail the action-set centred on the Jan Sangh candidate, but it was clear that it differed from that of his Congress opponent. Partly this was because, as I have said, the Jan Sangh candidate had gathered support over the past three years. He therefore had an action-set in which he was generally directly in contact with voters, or at the most stood at one remove from them. By contrast the Congress candidate started to work less than a month before the election. He could therefore make only superficial contacts with most voters, and had to rely on recruiting primary workers, who would then construct their own linkages. There were thus more intermediaries, and longer paths, in the Congress action-set.

This kind of comparison is connected to the analysis of election strategies.[13] I have elsewhere (Mayer, 1963, p. 126) distinguished between 'hard' and 'soft' campaigns in the Dewas elections. In the former, support is lined up at the start, and any attacks on prepared positions are rebuffed by the candidate or his workers, who keep especially close watch on the opposing

110

primary workers. In the latter, a drive at the end of the campaign is calculated to produce enough pressure to win, without the need for elaborate fence-mending among waverers and constant counter-bidding for those who sell their support in some way. In this ward, the Jan Sangh conducted the harder and the Congress the softer campaign. Now, it is possible to argue that an action-set with shorter paths will be more appropriate to a harder campaign. For any damage done by an opponent will be more quickly apparent to the candidate, who can then counteract it. The long-pathed set, on the other hand, would seem to be better for a softer campaign. For it involves a late drive by the largest number of supporters. Hence, whether by design or by their previous connection with the ward, the candidates' strategies and the pattern of their electoral action-sets can be correlated.

Another basis for comparison is the number of lateral links. By lateral link is meant a connection between intermediaries without reference to either ego or the terminal respondents. Lateral links are defined in terms of relevance to the criterion governing the formation of the action-set. In this case, then, only the lateral links connected with ego's election are relevant. This is not to deny, of course, that there are many lateral *network* ties linking people in the action-set, which are not used by ego or his intermediaries to achieve their ends. We must distinguish between the potential material of network links, and those links which are actually used in the action-set's constitution. The lateral linkage in an action-set does not indicate the complete pattern of interaction between members. For instance, in our diagram (p. 107) there is only one lateral linkage (between *A* and *B*) in terms of ego's recruitment of votes; yet, there would have been very many in terms of general interaction, notably those between all the people who were directly linked to the candidate as members of the Congress party. But these latter connections did not appear to recruit voters directly,[14] and so are not relevant to this action-set.

Lateral linkages can be contrasted with what might be called the multipronged linkage. This occurs when a respondent is linked to several intermediaries and possibly directly to ego as well. It differs from the lateral link, which is between intermediaries themselves. An example of a multipronged linkage in the action-set I have described would be the approach by several people to the Bagri voters (marked *C*). In terms of outward content, the lateral linkage brings several pressures to bear on an intermediary to approach the respondent, whereas the multipronged linkage brings several pressures to bear on the terminal respondent himself.

Clearly, the pattern of lateral and multipronged connections will reflect a difference in electoral campaigns. One might speculate, for example, that the part of the electorate at which the greatest number of prongs are pointed is the part which has the critical votes in the election. This would certainly be true as regards the Bagri vote in this ward, for it provided the balance of victory and was notoriously fickle. One might also suggest that the candidate with the action-set having the greatest number of lateral linkages is operating the strongest campaign, since intermediaries who might find a single inducement inadequate for their support are fortified by a second incentive coming to them laterally. The matter clearly needs further research; for one could also say that an action set in which no lateral ties exist is one in which loyalties must be firm enough not to require reinforcement. Such an analysis of action-sets could help to examine these and similar hypotheses on the nature of political process.

Another example of the comparative and explanatory value of the action-set comes from an investigation of the content of its linkages. This reveals that linkages exist because they carry transactions furthering in some way the interests of the parties concerned. The interest of the transactor is the same in each case – it is the interest of the ego around whom the action-set has formed (in my example, the interest of his election). The interest of the respondent can vary, ranging from specific aims to be fulfilled immediately after the election (such as help in arranging a marriage), to a generalized interest of potential help of some sort in the future.

This transactional element distinguishes action-set linkage from network linkage. True, persons linked in a network may derive some benefit from their relationships; but this is not because of the very nature of the relationship, and many of these relationships have an only minimally interactional aspect, a fact which prompted Firth's (1954, p. 4) caution when considering their part in defining the network.

In the Dewas example, the transactional element distinguishes the linkages of the action-set from other contacts between candidate and electorate. As I have said, the candidate personally met most of the voters in the ward in the course of his canvassing tours. These meetings were, it is true, transactional in the widest sense of the word; for the candidate would ask for support in return for promises to improve the roads, the water supply, etc. But such appeals to the voter were made publicly, and were made in the same terms to *all* voters. The support given through the linkages in the diagram, on the other hand, were specific to an individual or, at most, a few people. The campaign, therefore, contained activities at two levels: one was a public level, at which promises were given to the general electorate as part of the party's stated programme; the other was the private level, at which the promises given, and obligations encashed, were not necessarily connected with the party's programme for the Municipality. The first could be called diffusely and the second specifically transactional.

These two kinds of contact with electors can be used to distinguish different types of candidate and electoral campaign. In Dewas, for example, there were clear examples of both specifically and diffusely transactional candidates. The latter were mainly concerned with appealing to all sections of the electorate, and therefore phrased their campaign in non-partisan terms, promising to do their best for the ward. The former made no public speeches at all, as far as I could ascertain, and went on few canvassing expeditions in the ward. Instead, they concentrated on recruiting a number of allies who would each bring a few voters with him. The further analysis of why particular candidates operated a particular type of campaign will tell us more about small-town politics and politicians.

A study of action-set linkages in Dewas reveals two types of specific transaction, namely, those of patronage and brokerage. In the first, the transactor has the power to give some benefit which the respondent desires; upon fulfilment of the latter's part the benefit is made available. Examples of this would be the improvement of a road near the respondent's house, or the employment of the respondent (or his relative) in an office over which the transactor has control. The number and extent of such benefits naturally vary with the power of the transactor; but even the most influential is unlikely to be able to please everyone who comes to him, or who needs to be brought into the action-set. He must therefore husband these direct patronage transactions so that they produce linkages with key people who can bring followers with them.

Patronage resources are thus not unlimited; and patronage is an unambiguous transaction, in which the responsibility for any failure to redeem a promise can be clearly put down to the patron. The brokerage transaction differs somewhat in both these respects. A broker is a middle-man, and the transaction is one in which he promises to obtain favours for the respondent from a third person. Thus, brokers are intermediaries for the favours of government officials, or they have influence with powerful townsmen and are said to be able to expedite the business of the respondent. The ultimate responsibility for action rests not on the broker, however, but rather on the person to whom he has access. Clearly, the broker cannot maintain his reputation if too many of his efforts are unsuccessful; but at least some failures can be explained away by putting the blame on his contact. Hence, the broker can enter into more transactions, in relation to his resources of power, than can the patron. Both may make what turn out to be campaign promises at election time; but the broker has greater possibilities of doing so, since the patron will often be inhibited by unfulfilled promises of the past, or the fear of over-extending his activity.

Though these two types of transaction may overlap in practice, and though (as I have said) not all respondents have specific and immediate interests in mind, the distinction helps to explain the linkages of an action-set and their patterning. For instance, the patrons in an action-set may not deal directly with clients, finding it advantageous to shield themselves through intermediary brokers. One may, therefore, expect to find action-sets with longer paths of linkages where there are the more powerful patrons – other things being equal. This may be a reason why the Congress action-set in the diagram had longer paths than did the Jan Sangh action-set in the same ward (as I have noted). For Congress, as the ruling party, held greater powers of patronage in its hands.

ACTION-SET AND QUASI-GROUP

I believe that these examples show the value of the action-set concept in the study of political activities. How is it related to the concept of the quasi-group and what value does this approach have for the study of complex societies?

The action-set exists in a specific context which provides the terms of ego's purpose in forming linkages. When successive action-sets are centred on similar contexts of activity, personnel and linkages may also be similar. By 'superimposing' a series of action-sets, therefore, one may discern a number of people who are more often than not members of the action-sets, and others who are involved from time to time. Taken together, these people form a catchment for ego's action-sets based on this type of context. It is this potential membership which Bott calls a network; for all the people in any family's (or individual's) networks are not recruited on every occasion, but are possible members. Again, Epstein's network is of this sort, and he distinguishes between its effective and extended membership. I have already said why I do not consider network to be a very happy term here. Set is less confusing; it fits into Barnes's terminology and I have talked of classificatory and interactive sets at the start of this paper. But I think it may be well to adopt the word quasi-group, since this best expresses the sociological implications of this type of collection of people and suggests the qualitative difference between the quasi-group and the group.

The quasi-group, then, has the same pattern of linkages as the action-set, and exists through a series of contexts of activity without any formal basis for membership. The people who are more constantly involved in the successive action-sets need not be those closest to ego. It is possible to conceive of a supporter of a candidate in successive elections who is recruited through paths composed of different and transient inter-mediaries. However, when the more constant members *are* at

115

the same time those directly linked to ego, one can characterize them as the 'core' of the quasi-group. This core may later crystallize into a formal group; in the example I have given, this might involve the starting of a ward branch of the Congress party, to which those core members resident in the ward would belong. If it does not become a formal group, it can be seen to be a clique. This is a body of informally linked people, having a high rate of interaction and with that 'even spread' of membership activities which I have said distinguishes the group from the quasi-group. Though possessing leaders, cliques are not ego-centred bodies.[15] Where there is a clique at the centre of the quasi-group, it is possible for different egos, as members of the clique, to evoke the same pattern of linkages in different action-sets having similar contexts, and even in different contexts. Thus, where the core becomes a formal group or a clique, it may be possible to take it, rather than an individual, as the central ego – as Bott takes the whole family, rather than any single member, as her central unit.

It is clear that quasi-groups can be found in many arenas of social activity. In politics, for instance, a succession of action-sets of the kind we have seen to exist in Dewas would add up to form a quasi-group which could be called a faction. For, according to one view,[16] factions are units of conflict activated on specific occasions rather than maintained by a formal organization. They are 'loosely ordered' and with 'structurally diverse' bases of recruitment, and they are made manifest through a linkage of personal authority between leader and follower.[17] They are also based more on transactions than on issues of principle (Mayer, 1961, pp. 135-136), and may have groups or cliques as cores.

One way to study factions is to analyse the action-sets which make them up, focusing on such features as the size of core and periphery, the nature of the outward content of linkages, and the lengths of paths in various situations. From this could be built up a picture of the developmental cycle of factions, since an analysis of the content and pattern of linkages and their correlation with rivalries may reveal to us more about the critical point at which factions split.[18] From such a study would come a greater understanding of political situations involving quasi-groups rather than organized political units.

Quasi-groups also exist in the economic sphere, as an example from Dewas shows. Each of the sub-district towns, and the headquarters of Dewas, is concerned with the purchase of crops and their export from the District. This is done in officially supervised markets, where crop dealers buy from farmers. How do these dealers recruit and maintain their customers? Here, again, we can see action-sets, with the dealer as the central ego. For it is he who recruits a following with an 'inward' linkage based in each case on economic advantage, but with an 'outward' linkage resting on many criteria, including those of locality and common subcaste. We cannot say that all farmers dealing with a particular trader form a group; but since each is aware that many others (some of whom he knows) deal with the same trader they form an action-set at each harvest. Over a succession of harvests, there is some variation in the composition of the action-sets, since there is no compulsion to continue to deal with a particular trader. Nevertheless, there is also a continuity[19] within which a quasi-group is built up – one could call it a clientele. These clienteles can be studied in much the same way as I have suggested for political quasi-groups.

In the field of kinship, too, one can discern quasi-groups. In Central Indian peasant society, for example, a person has a number of kin whom he calls on for help in his affairs. I have called this the kindred of co-operation (Mayer, 1960, p. 4); one might characterize it as a quasi-group formed from a succession of action-sets centred on the individual or his household. Again, in talking of Iban society, Freeman distinguishes between the *de jure* kindred which constitutes a field of cognatic relations, and the *de facto* relationships of moral obligation which a man activates within this field and which form a major basis for recruitment to action-groups containing mainly cognatic kin though also including affines and friends (Freeman, 1961, pp. 202-211).[20] These action-groups sometimes appear to be organized groups (e.g. the travelling groups), but on other occasions seem to correspond to the action-sets I have described, and repeated recruitment might well produce a quasi-group.

The action-sets made up of kin are not mutually exclusive. Kindreds of cooperation form a series of overlapping collections

117

of people and an individual belongs to many at once, as he would not belong to different political factions or clienteles – an exception to this would be where two kinsmen are in opposition and recruit kin as supporters. Again, the outward content of recruitment is always at least partly one of kinship and its entailed moral obligations, whatever other incentives there may be to support ego; hence the content of linkages is less heterogeneous than it is in other action-sets. Thus we should perhaps see the kin-based quasi-group as a special and more restricted form.

More study is needed of this question, as well as of many others. For instance, what are the circumstances surrounding the emergence of cores and the part they play in the operation of the quasi-group; or what are the influences of space and time on quasi-groups? Again, what are the possibilities of making action-sets more easily comparable? One could, for example, tabulate the content of the first, second, third, etc., links along paths; one could also distinguish paths with different numbers of links, and thereby attempt to present a picture of the action-set without a cumbersome diagram of the kind I have presented. Quantification must, however, adequately express the total configuration, rather than merely categorize the properties of single links and paths; if this can be done, action-sets and consequently quasi-groups can be more easily compared.

CONCLUSION

I have attempted in this paper to see whether certain concepts may not be fruitful for social anthropologists. The identification of the action-set and the quasi-group owes much, of course, to the sociometric approach; it is also connected to analyses of other informal collections of people, such as cliques. Again, the action-set can be seen in terms of status- and role-sets (Merton, 1957, p. 368 et seq.). For a person as an ego has a role-set composed of relations towards intermediaries and terminal respondents; and as an intermediary he has a role-set comprising roles towards ego, respondents and perhaps further intermediaries. At a different level, ego and his intermediaries, and the intermediaries and the respondents, are linked by roles chosen from their status-sets. That is, an ego or an intermediary in a Dewas election will choose roles from the role-sets of caste, party, trade union, or from other role-sets in his status-set to attract followers. These two levels are connected with the inward and outward content of action-set linkages respectively.

The title of this paper suggests that I should discuss to what extent these concepts have particular reference to the study of complex societies. But, quite apart from a reluctance to involve myself in an effort to distinguish between complex and simple societies, I suggest that the action-set and the quasi-group are concepts which may apply in *any* situation where no organized groups operate. It is therefore relatively unimportant to assess whether they are more useful in complex than in simple societies. If indeed there are action-sets among, say, the Iban, one clearly cannot restrict the discussion to complex societies. Yet if one defines simple and complex societies as more and less involute (Nadel, 1957, p. 68) systems of role-relations, one might expect social relations in simpler societies to be more likely to be those of common group membership than they are in societies where there is a greater scatter of roles. If this be so, then the organizing of people in a simpler society will be more likely to bring together people with common group membership;[21] thus, in a given context, a sub-group will be more likely to form than an action-set.

Whether or not this be true, I have myself found that an approach of the kind I have outlined presented itself to me in the 'complex situation' of the Dewas election. It may well be that, as social anthropologists become more interested in complex societies and as the simpler societies themselves become more complex, an increasing amount of work will be based on ego-centred entities such as action-sets and quasi-groups, rather than on groups and sub-groups. This paper, therefore, is an attempt to explore and clarify the concepts involved, by applying them to an actual situation.

Adrian C. Mayer

NOTES

1. Ginsberg (1934, p. 40). Such quasi-groups are noted in field research too (e.g. Sower, 1957, p. 276). See also the use of the term 'collectivity' in this connection (Merton, 1957, p. 299).
2. I am indebted to Dr P. H. Gulliver for this term.
3. One must emphasize that a network is, of course, bounded by the total population which is being examined, or by the discontinuities in social relations produced by its own criteria. Hence, the 'unboundedness' is only relative.
4. Cf. the introduction of the term 'chain' by Moreno (1953, p. 720) as 'an open series of mutual choices on any criterion'.
5. A printer's error makes Bott (1957, p. 59) misquote Barnes as saying 'The image I have is of a net of points . . .'.
6. In saying that Barnes calls it a network when a person 'is in touch with a number of people, some of whom may be in touch with each other, and some of whom may not', Epstein (1961, p. 56) takes only the first part of Barnes's characterization; but this continues, 'each person has a number of friends and these friends have their own friends; some of any one person's friends know each other, others do not' (Barnes, 1954, p. 43). The difference here is between a finite set and an 'unbounded' entity.
7. Cf. the matrix of interrelated pairs constructed by Truman from voting records in the U.S. Congress, within which can be discerned the clusters which he calls blocs (Truman, 1959).
8. Research was conducted in 1960-1961 with the generous aid of the School of Oriental and African Studies, University of London.
9. For simplicity's sake, I have not shown the direct influence people acting as intermediaries may have on voters, but have marked only their links with others in the path itself.
10. I have called all links based on common subcaste 'kin' ties, since the people involved were all more or less distantly related; they are distinct from ties based on the membership of two subcastes in a caste, which I have called 'caste' ties.
11. When asked whether this pledge would be redeemed after the election, another Congress supporter cynically remarked that the issue would never arise. For Bagris would forgo Rajput status if it were pointed out to them that the considerable benefits they now received as a Backward Class would cease forthwith.
12. As Bott (1957, p. 58) says, 'In an organized group, the component individuals make up a larger social whole with common aims, interdependent roles, and a distinctive sub-culture. In network formation on the other hand, only some, not all, of the component individuals have social relationships with one another.'
13. I use this word in its popular, rather than in its game theory, meaning (see Snyder, 1955, p. 79).
14. A large number of links in the diagram are based on statements made by the interested parties to me or to other people in my hearing. Others are the results of my own observations and inferences, and of third-person information. In both cases, there may be other reasons for the actions of people, since it is impossible to know whether motives have been adequately assessed.

120

15. One must distinguish between those cliques formally recognized by the people themselves (e.g. those dealt with in Whyte, 1955) and those which the observer isolates. Loomis & Beegle (1950, p. 141) provide an example of the latter, in which there is an almost comprehensive series of linkages between clique members and an almost complete discontinuity of relations with the outside.
16. For another approach, see Siegel and Beals (1960).
17. Firth (1957, p. 292), summing up the conclusions of a symposium on factions.
18. For instance, my diagram shows that one of ego's close supporters has almost as many radiating linkages as ego himself. How far can splits be predicted where the linkages of supporters outnumber those of ego?
19. This is due in part to the contracting of debts with the dealer; hence there is less mobility than might be the case were the action-set to rest solely on the price offered by the dealer.
20. Freeman limits the kindred to cognatic kin, excluding affines. I have myself included the latter in my definition (and see Mitchell, 1963, p. 351). The issue here is not a terminological one, however, but one of the constitution of the action-sets and quasi-groups formed from these ties.
21. As Merton (1957, p. 311) puts it, 'in less differentiated societies, group affiliation tends to engage a considerably larger share of each member's personality'.

REFERENCES

BARNES, J. A. 1954. Class and Committees in a Norwegian Island Parish. *Human Relations* 7: 39-58.

BOTT, E. 1957. *Family and Social Network*. London: Tavistock Publications.

CHAPPLE, E. D. & COON, C. S. 1947. *Principles of Anthropology*. London: Cape.

EPSTEIN, A. L. 1961. The Network & Urban Social Organisation. *Rhodes-Livingstone Institute Journal* 29: 29-62.

FIRTH, R. W. 1954. Social Organisation & Social Change. *Journal of the Royal Anthropological Institute* 84: 1-20.

—— 1957. Factions in Indian & Overseas Indian Societies: Introduction. *British Journal of Sociology* 8: 291-295.

FREEMAN, J. D. 1961. On the Concept of the Kindred. *Journal of the Royal Anthropological Institute* 91: 192-200.

GINSBERG, M. 1934. *Sociology*. London: Butterworth.

LANCASTER, L. 1961. Some Theoretical Problems in the Study of Family & Kin Ties in the British Isles. *British Journal of Sociology* 12: 317-333.

LOOMIS, C. P. & BEEGLE, J. A. 1950. *Rural Social Systems*. New York: Prentice-Hall.

Adrian C. Mayer

MAYER, A. C. 1960. *Caste & Kinship in Central India*. London: Routledge & Kegan Paul.

—— 1961. *Peasants in the Pacific: A Study of Fiji Indian Rural Society*. London: Routledge & Kegan Paul.

—— 1962. System & Network: An Approach to the Study of Political Process in Dewas. In T. N. Madan & G. Sarana (eds.), *Indian Anthropology*. Bombay: Asia.

—— 1963. Municipal Elections: A Central Indian Case Study. In C. H. Philips (ed.), *Politics & Society in India*. London: Allen & Unwin.

MERTON, R. K. 1957. *Social Theory & Social Structure* (Rev. Edn.). Glencoe, Ill.: Free Press.

MITCHELL, W. E. 1963. Theoretical Problems in the Concept of Kindred. *American Anthropologist* **65**: 343-354.

MORENO, J. L. 1953. *Who Shall Survive? Foundations of Sociometry, Group Psychotherapy & Sociodrama*. Beacon: Beacon House.

NADEL, S. F. 1957. *The Theory of Social Structure*. London: Cohen & West.

RADCLIFFE-BROWN, A. R. 1952. *Structure & Function in Primitive Society*. London: Cohen & West.

SIEGEL, B. J. & BEALS, A. R. 1960. Conflict and Factional Dispute. *Journal of the Royal Anthropological Institute* **90**: 107-117.

SNYDER, R. C. 1955. Game Theory & the Analysis of Political Behaviour. In S. K. Bailey *et al.*, *Research Frontiers In Politics & Government*. Washington: Brookings Institution.

SOWER, C. *et al.* 1957. *Community Involvement: The Webs of Formal & Informal Ties That Make for Action*. Glencoe, Ill.: Free Press.

TRUMAN, D. B. 1959. *The Congressional Party: A Case Study*. New York: Wiley.

WHYTE, W. F. 1955. *Street Corner Society*. Chicago: Chicago University Press.

Ronald Frankenberg

British Community Studies
Problems of Synthesis

I

INTRODUCTION: AIMS

A recent survey of social status in British local communities lists twenty-one such communities studied since 1939 (Plowman *et al.*, 1962). Since this survey was published further studies have appeared of housing estates, a North Wales parish, a Devon village, and a Scottish border village (Collison, 1963; Emmett, 1964; Glass, R., 1964; Jennings, 1962; Littlejohn, 1964; Spencer, 1964; Williams, W. M., 1963; Willmott, 1963; Wilson, 1963). Other studies are known to be in preparation. Although few of these studies are by trained social anthropologists, all have been influenced by their work. It therefore seems to me useful to take stock of British community studies in a number of ways.

First, I intend to ask what kind of contribution concepts developed in the course of community studies can make to the general development of social anthropology as comparative sociology. Second, I wish to discuss briefly an attempt I am making in more detail elsewhere (Frankenberg, 1966) to relate British community studies to one another in order that they may both illuminate classical and modern sociological theories and themselves be illuminated by these. This task seems to me especially worthwhile because of the attitude of some orthodox sociologists towards community studies. Bottomore, for example, in his otherwise excellent book, makes virtually no use of community studies despite his own earlier excursion into the field. (Bottomore, 1954, 1962). C. Wright Mills's strictures on milieu studies (1959, see also Gerth & Landau, 1959) have been taken by his followers as valid criticisms of community studies and as reasons for not taking them seriously. From within the ranks of social anthropology, Freedman has recently made a

123

devastating attack. Writing of Radcliffe-Brown in China, Freedman says that he argued

'the most suitable unit of study was the village, both because most Chinese live in villages and because it was possible for one or two field workers to make a fairly detailed study in a year or so. According to Lin-yueh-hwa who sat at his feet in China, Radcliffe-Brown said that the best way to begin the study of Chinese social structure was to select a very small "social area", examine it meticulously, compare it with other specimens studied in the same manner, and then proceed to draw generalizations. It would seem that from this patient induction from studies of small social areas would emerge a picture of the social system of China. Of all the biases to which the anthropological approach has been subject this seems to me to be the most grievous. It is the anthropological fallacy *par excellence*' (Freedman, 1963, p. 3).

If Radcliffe-Brown expected a picture of the social system to *emerge* from such studies he was indeed deluded. Important generalizations however can be *drawn* out of them albeit with the aid of history and sociology. Sometimes such studies are held to be unrepresentative and therefore uninteresting. It is, of course, true as far as Britain is concerned that the majority of the population live in large towns and conurbations, whereas most of the studies with which I am concerned have been carried out in rural areas or in small towns. The characteristic feature of such 'communities' is their multiplicity of overlapping relationships. Indeed, where students in the anthropological tradition have turned their attention to large towns or segments of these, it is precisely such *gemeinschaftlich* relationships that they have sought. My third aim in this paper therefore will be to suggest an approach whereby what is positive in an anthropological approach can be applied to the study of social life in the characteristic unit of urban industrial society – the city.

I start from the view that what is positive about British social anthropology has been its emphasis on processes of change. Even at its most structural this emphasis has remained. It is partly dictated by the acceptance of a method of research which is at the least based on direct if not on participant observation (cp. Firth, 1951, pp. 18-19). This emphasis seems to me to be in sharp contrast with much twentieth-century British empirical sociology. Thus Evans-Pritchard in *The Nuer* sets out to give an analysis in structural terms of Nuer political organization. To do this he describes the process by which Nuer segments undergo fission and fusion. This model is a dynamic one, albeit a model of dynamic equilibrium rather than progressive change. In *The Sanusi of Cyrenaica* (Evans-Pritchard, 1949), moreover, he adds an historical element to his analytical method. On the other hand, consider the work of D. V. Glass, whose influence on generations of British sociologists parallels Evans-Pritchard's in the sister discipline. He sets out in his major work *Social Mobility in Britain* to describe a process. His methods and the nature of his material lead him to the categorization of static strata and the description of the structural framework in which mobility operates.

My concern is to see how social anthropologists might retain their process approach while invading the research area of the sociologist of urban industrial society. In this I do not mean to diminish the value of Glass's work nor that of his pupils but to supplement their achievements by adding another dimension.

II

CONCEPTS FROM MICROSOCIOLOGY

1. *Spiralism*

I will start with two examples of concepts derived from small-scale community studies which can add that dimension. The first comes from W. Watson. As a result of his experience in writing an unpublished study of the Scottish mining town of Buckhaven and later in considering the material collected by Birch and his collaborators on Glossop (Birch, 1959), Watson coined the term 'spiralists' to cover those individuals in society who were taking part in a process of 'progressive ascent . . . through a series of higher positions in one or more hierarchical structures' with a 'concomitant residential mobility through a number of communities' (Watson, 1964).

He also applies the term, 'burgesses' to those middle-class citizens of British towns and villages who are 'local' rather than

Ronald Frankenberg

'cosmopolitan' (Merton, 1957a, pp. 387-420) and whose families have dominated the high-street trade and local politics for two, three, or four generations. Spiralists seek their orientation to society through reference groups in firms, organizations, or professional associations which are not locally based. This may change when their career of promotion comes to an end and they become what Watson calls blocked spiralists. Watson's concepts promise a useful framework for the analysis of relationships between local and national systems. Even their brief exposition in a magazine article led to their use by Anthony Sampson in his attempt to describe British society as a whole (Sampson, 1962, p. 461; Watson, 1960).

2. *The stranger: science in wartime*
A second concept derived from the British local community study is my own elaboration of the concept of 'stranger'. I wrote in 1957, speaking of a North Wales village:

'Finally, in nearly every group activity, it is possible to recognize someone who has only that activity in common with the other members of the group or is a deviant in some respect from the distinguishing criteria of the group mainly concerned. Such a person, as I shall show, is to some extent removed from the conflicts and social pressures of full members of the group. This makes him or her of central importance in the precipitation and resolution of such conflicts' (Frankenberg, 1957, p. 44).

This view is, I think, capable of wider development and I have hinted at comparisons with African phenomena. (Cp. also Harris, 1961; I restate it here because in two recent books my usage has been misunderstood – Williams, 1963, p. 204; Emmett, 1964, p. 119.)

I have also found the notion of the stranger useful in re-analysing the wartime Lindemann-Tizard controversy over the Strategic Air Offensive (Snow, 1961, 1962; Frankenberg, 1963). The argument can be summarized by stating the two situations side by side.

The village had to maintain unity, though there were divided interests within it. The principal social division was that

126

between men and women and it was illustrated in their attitudes towards village football. The men's interest was in football as an independent activity which by its external success brought prestige to each as a representative of the village. The women's interest was in football as an auxiliary activity within the village which brought prestige to the individual through son or husband who acquitted himself well. When events outside committees made the recognition of this conflict of interests unavoidable, decisions were taken which threatened the interests of one group. They were legitimated by blaming them on strangers.

The Chiefs of Staff Committee was responsible to the Prime Minister for the overall conduct of the war. It had to maintain unity and co-operation between the services, but there were divided interests within it. The principal division was that between the Air Staff and the Naval Staff. The Air Staff were in favour of the use of independent air power for a strategic offensive. The Naval Staff were convinced that the most valuable use of air power was as a tactical auxiliary in the sea battle of the Atlantic. When situations arose where the conflict came into the open the respective chiefs of staff used stranger scientists and mathematical myths to express viewpoints and legitimate decisions which in fact were largely effected by the relative political power of Air Ministry and Admiralty and by external events (cp. Devons, 1950).

I think the same analogy can be used with profit elsewhere in considering the social situations surrounding the roles played by psychiatrists in British courts, rate-fixers in industry, and business consultants (cp. Parkinson, 1960).

While both the concepts of 'spiralism' and of the 'stranger' show ways in which insight derived from local studies may be applied to studies of a very different kind, on their own they do not achieve the synthesis of the particular into the general, 'the parochial into the oecumenical' (Merton, 1957a) which is desirable. To sketch out an approach to this, it is necessary to describe briefly the studies of British local communities which are available.

III

BRITISH COMMUNITY STUDIES: A FIELD SURVEYED

The pioneer study in the British Isles was, of course, that of Arensberg and Kimball in the Irish countryside of County Clare, describing the social life of small farmers in a subsistence farming area. This study was completed in the thirties and published just before the Second World War. (Arensberg & Kimball, 1948; Arensberg, 1937). Among their major achievements were: (a) the analysis of the effects of rural debt between equals as maintaining through reciprocal ties the social organization of the countryside; and (b) the part played by the 'match' and marriage in maintaining family and community.

The next study to be done in order of time was Alwyn Rees's *Life in a Welsh Countryside*, again concerned with social life and among near-subsistence farmers on marginal land. As Peters (personal communication) has pointed out, a remarkable feature of this study is Rees's demonstration of the role of the young men's group. This group had a licensed joking relationship with the rest of the community which served to reinforce group norms. A pupil of Alwyn Rees, W. M. Williams, published the next major monograph, *Gosforth: The Sociology of an English Village*. Here, for the first time in a British rural study, a complicated system of social stratification was described, though once again, the emphasis was on agriculture and a group of family farms. In this parish, however there were many labourers, not only agricultural but also industrial, employed in a nearby atomic energy authority plant. Departing from chronological order, I mention next my own study, *Village on the Border* which dealt with a *village* rather than a *parish*. The men had formerly worked in slate and granite quarries, but after their closure most of the men found work in industry outside the village in nearby towns. There were also farms in the neighbourhood but my emphasis was on the village and the wage-earners and their wives who lived and worked and sometimes played in it. The Yorkshire mining town, pseudonymously called Ashton, was studied by Dennis, Henriques, and Slaughter (two anthropologists and a sociologist) at about the same time. The analytic focus of their *Coal is Our Life* was the relationship between the nature of work in the pits and other aspects of social life. They laid special emphasis on leisure, trade unionism, the family, and the extremely segregated roles of the sexes.

In the mid-nineteen-fifties also a political scientist with a group of collaborators from various disciplines set out to study political life in the small relatively isolated textile town of Glossop not far from their home university of Manchester (Birch, 1959). Another urban community study was Margaret Stacey's, *Tradition and Change*. This reported on a study of Banbury, a market and industrial town in Oxfordshire with a population of about 19,000. Of the various studies at present available this comes nearest to a microcosm of the nation – Britain writ small. Most types of industry and commerce are found in Banbury and there is a complete range of social classes and status groups.

The Irish and Welsh countryside, Gosforth, Pentrediwaith, Ashton, Glossop, and Banbury, the more recently studied Ashworthy, Llan and Westrigg are all relatively small and relatively compact territorial units. They are clearly spatially defined and delimited and of a type (with the possible exception of Banbury) which most scholars do not hesitate to call a community. After the Second World War Ruth Glass pioneered the study of Bethnal Green, a working-class district in the East End of London which has become the Iroquois of British urban ethnology (Glass, R. & Frenkel, 1946). The Institute of Community Studies is now within the area and from it Michael Young and his associates have produced a trilogy of local studies (Young & Willmott, 1957; Townsend, 1957; Marris, 1958, cp. also Robb, 1954). These studies continued a line of inquiry that had been started before the War, for Mrs Glass (as Durant, 1939) had earlier published a short but classic study of an urban housing estate, *Watling*. In it she examined the claims of Watling to be considered as a community, and outlined what has now become the familiar pattern of the rise and decline of leadership in community association and centre (Dennis, 1961). This study has had many successors.

Ronald Frankenberg

BRITISH COMMUNITY STUDIES: A CONTINUUM
SUGGESTED

The studies I have described and the more recent works cited
above do not form an exhaustive list but they provide the
principal raw material for the approach to synthesis which I
wish to attempt. I have listed them here in a roughly ordered
way which coincidentally is also almost chronological. The
sequence is from communities with a simple productive basis
such as truly rural subsistence farming, up through areas based
on extractive industry, manufacturing, and mixed economy
towns, to reach at last traditional and nontraditional sections
of great conurbations. There are, of course, gaps in the record
but there is a sense in which, as phylogeny is repeated in
ontogeny and both are reflected in the morphology of the
developed organism, so the development through time charted
by the social historian is paralleled in this social morphological
series. By arranging them in this way we can test the usefulness
of the historical hypotheses of the classical sociologists. We
cannot, of course, in this way, test the hypotheses themselves.
I have arranged modern extant British communities along a
typological continuum based on economic organization and on
technology.

I believe this approach is derived from that of Radcliffe-Brown
who wrote:

'The basis of science is systematic classification. It is the first
task of social statics to make some attempt to compare
forms of social life in order to arrive at classifications. But
forms of social life cannot be classified into species and genera
in the way we classify forms of organic life; the classification
has to be not specific but typological, and this is a more
complicated kind of investigation. It can only be reached by
means of the establishment of typologies for features of
social life or the complexes of features that are given in
partial social systems' (Radcliffe-Brown, 1952, p. 7).

V

CONCEPTS IN THE CONTINUUM

I believe it is possible to show (Frankenberg, 1966) an associated progression in the following terms, drawn respectively from, (*a*) classical sociology, (*b*) modern sociology, and (*c*) social anthropology.

1. *Concepts from classical sociology*
The first two terms I take from Durkheim.

(*a*) As we move from one end of the continuum to the other, relatively little division of labour changes into extreme differentiation and specialization. Here, of course, it has to be borne in mind that the scale within Britain is a very short one. As we shall see below, the division of labour has implications also for role theory.

(*b*) Durkheim associated this increasing division of labour with the move from mechanical to organic solidarity. Although his metaphor is confusing, the phenomenon which he is describing is clear enough. In the communities at the beginning of the scale, men and women work side by side with others in relatively self-sufficient units. In the conurbation each depends upon all and none can survive alone.

(*c*) Sir Henry Maine's description of the development from status to contract can also be applied to the continuum.

(*d*) Durkheim's historical view of a development in society from regional to occupational organization is reflected morphologically in the continuum. Banbury is central in this regard as the meeting-point of local and cosmopolitan worlds.

(*e*) Perhaps over familiar, is Tönnies's theory of the transition from 'community' to 'association', which can be accepted as having some valid application despite the overtones to which Williams draws attention (Williams, 1963, p. xvii) when he writes of it as 'a view of country life as fighting a subborn rearguard action against antagonistic external forces, perhaps urban in origin'.

(*f*) Weber's description of the historical processes of rationalization and bureaucratization also fits the continuum.

(*g*) Finally, among the relevant ideas to be drawn from

131

classical sociology, is Marx's view of the process of proletarianization. As I understand this, it implies a transition from
economic class as just one division among many to economic
class as dominating social life through the cash nexus. Marx and
Durkheim, and even Weber, saw social change as a more rapid
process than it has proved. Proletarianization is not complete
even in the segregated urban housing estate. Were it to be
completed, Marx's prediction of a total breakdown of social life
would become reality.

2. *Concepts from modern sociology*
(*a*) Among British social anthropologists, Nadel and Southall
have gone furthest in applying the concepts of modern sociology
(Nadel, 1951, 1957; Southall, 1959). They represent an approach
which fuses the sociological and the social anthropological
tradition. Southall, in particular, has been directly concerned
in the field of orthodox social anthropology with the sort of
typological problem that I am exploring here. He suggests that
what he terms 'the density of role texture' may change pro-
gressively along a rural-urban continuum. (I prefer to regard
the continuum I am presenting as a rural/non-rural scale since
it is based on much less thorough study of the urban than of
the rural.) Southall argues that as low population density gives
way to high population density, roles cease to splay across the
five major type categories he lists – kinship and ethnic, economic,
political, ritual and religious, and recreational. Roles become
specialized in one or other of these fields. Secondly as roles
become more narrow in their reference to particular areas of
social life, they also become less diffuse and more specific in the
behaviour described as appropriate to them. Father/employer/
ritual-leader/teacher becomes father and employer and priest
and teacher. In the traditional English countryside one must
plough and sow and reap and mow to be a farmer's boy.
Southall makes a third distinction between the overt role-
relationship at the rural end and latent role-relationship at the
other. Thus roles in the countryside are mediated by direct
face-to-face relationships. In the town – the roles of fellow-
members in a voluntary association may never bring their
incumbents face to face. This point is implied by Ruth Glass

(Glass, R., 1955). Thus the Banbury and Glossop studies, in contrast to those that precede them in the scale, are much concerned with voluntary associations, voting patterns, political and religious allegiances and prejudices. Finally, Southall points to what may be regarded as rural role democracy. Each individual in the countryside has equal access to roles which he can fill and to role-relationships which he can take part in. The stratification and above all spatial segregation of strata in the non-rural situation ensure that this is not the case.

(*b*) Southall does not exhaust the possible applications of the role concept to this field. People at the rural end of the continuum fill a small number of roles and hence have overlapping role-relationships. The bus-conductor may also be conductor of the choir and a cousin to his passengers. People in non-rural society may have more roles open to them, but they are filled in discrete situations.

(*c*) Merton's concept of the role-set (Merton, 1957) also has application here. Merton points out that roles are often part of a set, such as, for example, teacher, pupil, head, school governor, parent. In such a role set, each role-other may have different role-expectations in relation to the teacher. The incumbent of the teacher-role can only succeed in meeting these conflicting expectations if the situation lacks what Merton calls 'transparency'. That is to say, it is necessary that one role-other should neither witness nor know of the teacher's behaviour to another role-other in the set. Transparency is more likely to arise in the rural than in the non-rural situation. This gives rise to special conflict-reducing rituals and practices in the rural area. In the non-rural area the·same is achieved by spatial and social segregation.

(*d*) A reading of Goffman's paper 'Role Distance' (1961) suggests a further dimension to the continuum. He distinguishes between role commitment, role attachment, and role embracement with each term here including its predecessors. People in rural society are committed to their roles by restricted geographical and social mobility. The transparency of small-scale society may make it inevitable that they are both embraced by and embrace their roles. As unforeseen role possibilities emerge out of increasing integration with wider society, they may become merely attached or just committed. The social and geographical mobility permitted by large-scale society may make possible the avoidance even of commitment.

(*e*) Different aspects of status are dominant at the rural and non-rural ends of the continuum. Status at the rural end tends to be total and ascribed and at the other partial and achieved (cp. Plowman *et al.*, 1962, where a distinction is made between interactional rural and attributional urban status). This is closely related to the fact that at the rural end of the continuum status determines *how* people behave when they meet; at the non-rural end *whether* they meet at all! Also in this is associated the question of whether people are educated according to the status they have, or accorded status by the education they have received (Marshall, 1950).

(*f*) In an earlier part of the paper I referred to Merton's association of status and network in his distinction between local and cosmopolitan influentials. Cosmopolitan influentials are concerned with the quality of their networks rather than with the numbers of people involved. This affects the nature and scale of the set they can muster in exerting influence (cp. Mayer's essay in this monograph).

3. *Concepts from social anthropology*
(*a*) Elizabeth Bott and John Barnes (Bott, 1957; Barnes, 1954) have spelled out the differences between the contained, small-mesh, close-knit network of the rural community and the dispersed, large mesh, loose-knit network which the scale of non-rural society makes possible.

(*b*) From Radcliffe-Brown comes the idea that when relationships of disjunction and conjunction are present in the same social relation this gives rise to joking relationships. These are relatively more frequent in the countryside. They survive in non-rural areas only when segregation and hence avoidance are not possible, as for example in the class confrontations of factory and workplace (Bradney, 1957a, 1957b; Girling, 1957; following Radcliffe-Brown, 1952).

(*c*) Gluckman's distinction between complexity and complication and rebellion and revolution (Gluckman, 1954, 1955) are also relevant. Life in the small-scale community is governed by links between individuals which cut across and reinforce one another. As the individual grows into adulthood in rural society he takes more part in social life so that his ties to those around him are multiplied. In the non-rural society additional roles bring interaction with more people, each role-relationship carrying a simplex tie.

4. *A concept from outside: social redundancy*

I do not think I have exhausted the possibilities of variables which change along a morphological scale of communities arranged from economically simple to economically complex. Those I have listed can, for example, be seen as making up the changes which *may* tend towards the development to alienation and anomie seen by many writers since Marx and Durkheim. This, however, is to put too deterministic and inevitable an interpretation upon them. It is also to focus unduly upon the end-product – the least adequately studied town (for a critical view see Dennis, 1958). A formulation which seems to be useful is to borrow and adapt a term from communication theory – *social redundancy*. Cherry (1961) sees language as the resultant of two opposing tendencies. The one, the need to be brief tends to eliminate 'redundancy' in expression. The other, the need to be understood, promotes it. Similarly, communication networks may multiply channels in order to be sure that messages are received in spite of interfering 'noise' (Bell, 1962). Societies at the rural end of the scale show more redundancy in both senses but there is also a qualitative difference. Social redundancy does not disappear altogether as one moves along the continuum but it changes its form. The difference between spoken and written language provides a simple analogy:

'Conversation is built out of a relatively small vocabulary . . . but the words may be arranged with great fluidity into varied patterns with repetitions, stressings, gestures and a wealth of reinforcing "redundancy". Writing must make up for the lack of gesture or stress, if it is to combat ambiguity, by introducing redundancy through a wider vocabulary with a closer adherence to grammatical structure' (Cherry, 1961).

The parallel with the development of a rural/non-rural con-

tinuum seems close. Rural social life *is* built up out of a relatively
small number of role-relationships which *are* arranged with
great fluidity into varied patterns. As we move along the scale
a large number of formalized (alienated?) role-relationships
replace this fewness and fluidity.

VI

SOCIAL ANTHROPOLOGY: THE STUDY OF PROCESS

It is, I think, immediately apparent, especially to that majority
of social anthropologists who have studied at the rural end of
my continuum, that the different nature of 'partial societies'
at the other end of the scale make their study by anthropological
techniques difficult. The reaction of many will be to concentrate
on other fields. This is, I believe, to fail to make a contribution
for which social anthropologists are well qualified. It is to this
problem that I now wish to turn. How can social anthropologists retain that which I described earlier as their process
approach while invading the research area of the urban
sociologist?

1. *Two case studies: a North Wales and a South Wales village*
I can state the problem most clearly as it impinged on me in
attempting to study and compare the part played by the
organization of education in the social life of two Welsh villages.
The first case which I have called Pentrediwaith was a village
of some 600 people isolated in a rural valley of North Wales
(Frankenberg, 1957). It was a residential unit which had also
until recently been the centre of its inhabitants' working and
recreational lives. I was able, by attending a series of meetings
in the village and by conversations with villagers while living
in the village, to understand how villagers reacted to the
external constraints of the local education authority. I could
analyse events in terms of changing relationships between
individuals and groups. I could show how relationships in one
situation led to relationships in others and suggest ways in
which the village as a whole formed a system undergoing
processes of change. In this village differences of social alignment were openly expressed at public meetings. Divisions into

136

Church and Chapel, Welsh and English, villagers and outsiders, appeared in every aspect of daily life. In particular, I emphasize the villagers' ambivalent attitude to the Welsh language. They were both proud of it and unwilling to share it. Yet at the same time inability to speak English was a sign of lack of culture. They did not speak Welsh to, or even in front of, English-speaking villagers. The latter in turn were sometimes resentful of Welsh and suspicious almost to the point of paranoia if it was, by chance or design, spoken in their presence. It was not necessary, when describing events, to chart the divisions fully and in advance. They became evident in the description. Structure emerged from process.

The second village I studied was a larger one with about 2,000 inhabitants which formed part of the extensive industrial complex of the South Wales Coalfield. Its boundaries were less clearly defined in geographical, economic, and social terms. People who lived in this village worked elsewhere as a matter of course. Many had in the past travelled to London to live and work. Villagers sought recreation elsewhere, and often had as many links with non-villagers as with other villagers. Meetings about education here were less dramatic and groups with conflicting interests in the Welsh language avoided bringing a continuous process of conflict into the open by avoiding one another. There were divided views in this village about the relative desirability of the Welsh and English languages as media of instruction in the primary school. These views were not randomly or idiosyncratically distributed but the conflict of views represented a conflict of social groups.

2. *Language and education in South Wales*

A so-called 'Welsh School' was introduced into the village in 1954. The Welsh School movement, although started by a private person is a logical development of government bilingual policy. The idea is a simple one. It is argued that the best medium of instruction for infants and juniors (children under 12) is the language of their home. This presents no problem in those few areas which are either entirely Welsh-speaking or entirely English-speaking. In the more usual cases where there are substantial minorities of either English-speaking or Welsh-speaking families, the theory demands separate provision for each linguistic group. Children from English-speaking homes must be taught all subjects, including Welsh, through the medium of English. Children from Welsh-speaking homes must be taught all subjects, including English, through the medium of Welsh. It was for this last purpose, apparently both obvious and beneficial, that the 'Welsh School' was opened.

The social situation was more complex than the linguistic division might suggest. It is generally believed in the district at large that the village is a very Welsh place. The majority of the population in the central part of the village can and do speak Welsh although few of them read much in Welsh. Chapel services and religious meetings are conducted in Welsh, but political meetings and other social gatherings are conducted in English. Villagers do not have the emotionally charged attitude to the Welsh language that I have described for North Wales. No one ever hesitated to speak Welsh in front of me. During meetings if anyone spoke in Welsh they did so without bravado or embarrassment despite the presence of monoglot English speakers. They, again in contrast to the North Wales village, did not specifically draw attention to the fact that they were speaking Welsh and the English-speakers present showed no resentment. The Welsh language, despite its link with Chapel membership, is not in the second village a weapon of exclusion. It was the language of work and play until the Second World War. Many of the men who left the village temporarily during the economic depression of the late twenties and thirties, returned with English-speaking wives whom they had married in London. Even those who married Welsh girls while away adopted English as their language of courting and retained it after their marriage and return to the village. I knew couples who spoke Welsh to their friends, shopkeepers, and neighbours but English to each other and to their children.

Those families who habitually spoke Welsh and those who did not nevertheless both shared the feeling that in the Welsh language they had a valuable possession which ought to be preserved and passed on to their children. Opponents and supporters of the Welsh School were united in their belief that it was good for children to learn Welsh. Opponents of the school said their children could learn Welsh at Sunday School and at home. Some even gave their children's proficiency in Welsh as a reason for not sending them to the Welsh School. Others said that Welsh was all very well at home but that it was insufficiently commercial to learn at school. Some of these cited their own experiences in London or in the nearby steel-producing town of Port Talbot. They recalled the disadvantages they thought they had suffered because of their inadequate and badly pronounced English. They were, of course, misconstruing the aim of the Welsh School.

Welsh, then, may be valued as a possession but spoken as a matter of course. It was considered to be and was in fact the language of much village activity, of prayer, and of family life. Yet English was necessary if one was to get on. This last point is important because most villagers did not see their children's future as being confined within the village. Although the village represented an island of Welsh in a sea of English, and Welsh-speaking was in some sense a symbol of village solidarity, it did not, as in West and North Wales, represent working-class or *gwerin* (folk) solidarity. In the Port Talbot area in which the village lies, and in Eastern South Wales generally, the language of steelworks, pit, and trade union branch was emphatically English. Even in the most traditional part of the village the ward Labour party conducted most of its business in English; speakers, mainly those from outside the village, occasionally broke into Welsh, either from habit or to emphasize their informality.

In the central traditional part of the village there lived a small elite of literary minded Welsh speakers who read and wrote extensively in Welsh. They were sensitive about their spoken Welsh and were at pains to explain that it was not real Welsh but 'a sloppy way of speaking' peculiar to the village. They said they did not like to speak 'real Welsh' because neighbours and other villagers would think that they were putting on airs and trying to get above themselves. There was therefore no general drive among adult villagers to improve the standard of spoken Welsh. An attempt to run a Welsh class in the village failed.

When the idea of having a Welsh school was first mooted, it

was proposed from outside the village and by prominent national leaders. Questionnaires were sent to all parents in the valley and 300 said they would like their children to attend. The next move was not made until seven years later, this time by a county alderman, when it was the occasion for a stormy meeting. The discussion raged not about the principle but about whether pupils at a Welsh School stood as good a chance of successfully surmounting the next stage on the ladder to higher education – the so-called eleven-plus selection test for the grammar school. Despite the efforts of the two local Nonconformist preachers to persuade parents to send their children to the Welsh School, by the time it opened only 12 of the 95 available primary school children went to it. Its numbers were made up to 58 by children from neighbouring villages. It is evident that the Welsh school was not popular in the village. Many people had a Welsh and Chapel background which had led the school's supporters to believe that they would send their children there, but in the event they did not do so. The parents who did send their children included a high proportion of people in the higher-status occupations.

The situation was much discussed and it was generally argued by villagers that the successful campaign for a Welsh school had split the village. In fact it revealed that an underlying conflict of interests existed. But the nature of the village made it difficult to find situations in which this conflict became socially manifest. Opposing groups tended to be segregated both geographically within the village and socially by the meetings and chapels that they attended or failed to attend. (In this sense the South Wales village lies towards the non-rural end of the continuum I have described.) Some crucial occasions revealed conflict. In certain cases people were significantly absent and in others members of different social groups were brought into contact and hence open dispute. The original meetings referred to above occurred before I went to the village. Another potential occasion was the schools' annual St David's Day celebration traditionally held on 1 March. The organization of this in the village was typical – two celebrations were held. During the first year of the Welsh School's existence, one of the Nonconformist ministers attended only its St David's Day celebration. He was still being criticized for this a year later and there was speculation as to which school the ministers would attend in 1956. In the event each of the two ministers spent some time at each school.

The celebrations were held in the morning between ten and twelve o'clock, simultaneously in the two schools. At the Welsh School celebration which was held, significantly, in the vestry of the Baptist Chapel, there were between 60 and 75 women. There were also 6 ministers of various chapels in the district sitting together at the back of the hall. Each standard of the school performed in turn. They sang hymns and folk songs and performed action songs and dances in costume. They also acted two sketches. One of these was a panorama of the seasons. The other, the grand finale, was a pageant of Welsh folk heroes who came onto the stage in costume, announced themselves, and recited their achievements. The whole programme was in Welsh. The patriotic element was also present at the County Primary School but it was less marked. The attendance was much greater. There were more than 100 women present and three men – all Methodist deacons. In addition there were the headmaster, and the two local ministers who appeared occasionally from their attendance at the Welsh School. The programme consisted of a series of light songs and sketches culminating in a performance of *Aladdin*. Once again, the whole programme was in Welsh. When photographs of the Welsh school's performance and not of the other appeared in the *Western Mail* next day this could not cause more than informal grumbling and gossip which could find no formal outlet. Honours were even when the Welsh School had to wait a fortnight for the report in the *Port Talbot Guardian* which the County Primary had in the same week.

The only situation in which the conflict came into the open was at the village Eisteddfod. This was held annually under the auspices of both the Anglican church and the two Nonconformist chapels. It was held on a Saturday in two sessions, afternoon and evening. The afternoon was devoted to children's competitions both solo and in groups. I had been warned that jealousies between the parents were great and sometimes led to argument. The afternoon session in 1956 was conducted turn and turn about by the Baptist and Methodist ministers. It fell to the Baptist minister to introduce the competition for speaking of choral verse in Welsh for children under 12. There was only one party entered for this, that sent by the County Primary School. In the course of some general remarks about how regrettable it was that the entries were so few in this and other sections, the Minister referred to this party as 'Parti Ysgol Saesneg' – the English School Party. The headmaster of the County Primary, whose own child attended the Welsh School, was in the audience. He called out in Welsh, 'My school is not the English School, it's as Welsh as the other and it's been here longer'. The minister replied that he had meant nothing by calling it Ysgol Saesneg and if that was the sort of hostile spirit in which the proceedings were to be carried on, they might as well call it a day and go home. The meeting paused for some time in a general murmur of conversation and then the murmurs died down and the competitions continued. The incident passed and the overt hostility it had revealed and intensified was dispersed once more into informal gossip. It is important that the gossip was confined to friends and neighbours who did not differ on the issues at stake. Interaction did not cross lines of hostility except in formal terms and in formal situations.

Given a knowledge of the groupings within the village and the history of their differences, the examination of the crucial disturbance which broke down the segregation of village groups throws light on the processes of village life. Unfortunately, I was not sufficiently alert to its significance at the time to collect adequately detailed information.

VII

PROCESS IN URBAN RESEARCH: A DRAMATIC APPROACH

It points however to the possibility of drawing together four strands in the development of our subject to suggest a fruitful technique of urban research. These are, first, the growth of a 'dramatic' approach in British social anthropology, paralleled, second, by Merton's approach to functional analysis in sociology (Merton, 1957a, p. 60); third, by the development of a dramaturgical approach (Goffman, 1959, 1961; Stein, 1960); and finally by a reconsideration at a new level of technique of the methods of Mass Observation (Madge & Harrisson, 1939; Harrisson, 1961) so warmly commended by Malinowski (1938).

1. *The drama in events*

The focus on 'dramatic occurrences' as a line of development in British social anthropology has been commented on briefly by Gluckman in his foreword to Turner's *Schism and Continuity in an African Society* (1957) and by Barnes in his inaugural lecture in the University of Sydney (1958) (see also Gluckman, 1961). It may take the form of a case history of a specific incident, a type of incident or a series of incidents. An example of the first is Gluckman's use of a bridge-opening ceremony as a way into the analysis of the complexities of modern Zululand (Gluckman, 1940, 1942). The second is well illustrated by Mitchell's analysis of *The Kalela Dance*. Here Mitchell uses the existence of a particular pattern of ceremonialized behaviour and the detailed consideration of a particular team of dancers to illuminate the meaning of tribalism in an urban setting and to demonstrate its differences from traditional tribal ties (see also Pons, 1961, and especially Gluckman, 1955b). The most explicit development of the method lies, however, in Turner's use of the concept of social drama as a unit of analysis. In his words:

> 'The social drama is a limited area of transparency on the otherwise opaque surface of regular, uneventful social life. Through it we are enabled to observe the crucial principles of the social structure in their operation, and their relative dominance at different points of time' (1957, p. 93).

Turner's view of a social drama is a highly specific one in which a breach of social norms is followed in turn by a crisis, then redressive action and either reintegration or recognition of schism. He is concerned with successive levels of social conflict and the 'social mechanisms brought into play' to 'reduce, exclude or resolve that conflict'. His dramas all involve in the first instance open disruption of a temporarily achieved equilibrium.

Such situations may be difficult to observe in an urban

industrial environment. Much of urban life, however, depends (even more perhaps than rural) on the correct performance of ceremonial in the form of etiquette. The urban dweller is brought into daily contact with others who are strangers to him. He has means of categorizing them and then ways of behaving appropriate to each category. Goffman (1959), once again in a formulation arising out of experience in a community study, in the Shetlands, has suggested a way of looking at these daily encounters within a dramatic framework. Each individual (or group) presents himself in a particular light in a particular situation. If his definition of the situation is to prevail, there must be a working consensus with the others involved in the interaction about the definition of what is relevant and irrelevant to the encounter. In a later work (1961) he argues that the maintenance of any gathering focused on a particular activity (whether this is merely conversation, or a game or an elaborate ritual) involves tension arising from the determination of the participants to exclude that which they have defined as irrelevant. A happening which breaks down the barrier of irrelevance he calls an 'incident'. It leads to a redefinition of the limits of the encounter. This is a wider category of which breaches of the kind described by Turner are a special case. Such an approach means that the analysis of social dramas in urban society may cover a very short span of time. The Eisteddfod incident described above lasted for less than five minutes; the events at the opening of the bridge in Zululand less than one day. The implication is that minute and detailed observation is necessary and 'maps' of the disposition of participants have the importance in this kind of study that genealogies have in orthodox classical anthropology. Since the significance of the event is apparent only to a knowledgeable observer, traditional fieldwork methods are not as irrelevant as some recent writers seem to have suggested (Freedman, 1963, pp. 6-7).

Such studies, however, as Turner forcibly argues, must be put in the context of quantitative descriptive information on the society in which they take place. 'Before one can study breach one must be aware of regularities' (Turner, 1957, p. xvii). He continues to describe his own method of work:

'First, I have compared a number of villages with reference to such measurable criteria as size and genealogical composition. Secondly, I have analysed a sequence of social dramas involving the membership of a single village, and the members of other villages linked to it by ties of kinship and spatial propinquity. In the first instance, I have examined regularities of *form* occurring throughout *many* villages; in the second, I discuss regularities of *process* in the social maturation of a *single* village. The two approaches complement one another' (1957, pp. xvii-xviii).

These complementary approaches are freely available to the social anthropologist attracted to the study of British urban society, since the existence of a national census and the development of sophisticated statistical techniques provide much general information about towns and parts of towns (cp. Moser & Scott, 1961) which the field anthropologist in Africa has to collect for himself.

In some spheres the *form* of British society is well documented. The relationship of social class and status to family life, politics, and style of life is well known in general terms. There are however few detailed studies of individual events. Apart from my own very shallow description of events surrounding football and the carnival in Pentrediwaith (1957), there is little outside novels on the kind of crisis that Turner describes.

A different approach may be made through the detailed description and analysis of ceremonial events. An account has been presented of funerals in the Hebrides (Vallee, 1955), and a detailed analysis of a funeral in South Wales (Loudon, 1961). Less satisfactory but still welcome are descriptions of a marriage in Bethnal Green (Young & Willmott, 1957), a club night out in Ashton (Dennis *et al.*, 1956), and a council meeting in Glossop (Birch, 1959).

2. *The drama in ceremonial*
Recurrent ceremonial dramas open a second window onto opaque urban social process. For in such ceremonies, individuals and groups, normally segregated, temporarily come into interaction. Examples are:

(*a*) Ceremonials surrounding individual and family life crises – such as christenings, weddings and funerals and (*b*) reactions to individual tragedies such as 'whiprounds' after fire, flood, and accident.

(*c*) Perennial occurrences such as Christmas, Easter, bank holidays, holidays in general, elections, and meetings.

(*d*) Occasional celebrations such as Coronations, victory parades, etc (cp. Jennings & Madge, 1937).

To study the dramatic event is not necessarily to ignore the normal, as Malinowski pointed out in his comments on Mass Observation's emphasis on just the themes I have listed above (Malinowski, 1938, p. 108). After pointing to this organization's emergence during the Abdication Crisis and its study of the Coronation and of Armistice Day, Malinowski continues:

> 'These factors are sufficient to show that those who are directing the movement realise the unique value of such occasions. Such a recognition need not of course exclude an equal interest in the normal events of every day, and the essential data for the study of the play of social relations undisturbed by crisis. The normal is far more difficult to penetrate than the exceptional, but it is equally important. The close study of such exceptional situations, however, may give the clue to much that is baffling in the uniform and impassive surface of everyday things.'

3. *The drama in custom*

More recently, Fortes (comment on Eisenstadt, 1961, p. 211) has suggested that the concern of anthropologists in Britain who wish to apply a Malinowskian model should be a return to the study of custom. He instanced the study of customs surrounding Christmas. This seems to me acceptable in terms of the 'continuum' and 'dramatic' approaches I have outlined. Christmas is an international festival but the details of its celebration vary from country to country and from place to place within Britain. A detailed study of Christmas celebrations in a number of selected towns and villages might be as revealing of the place of religion in social life as more extensive social surveys, if indeed not more revealing. It would have to be set in a framework of national and historical data. In each case Merton's protocol (Merton, 1957a, p. 60) for functional analysis could usefully be applied. The deficiencies of the Mass Observation surveys show what may be expected when such a conceptual framework is lacking. Each incident needs to be examined in terms of at least five kinds of factor. First, from which categories of the total population that could take part are the actual participants drawn? Are they, for example, men or women, high status or low status? How are they related to one another and to others not participating? Second, what are they not doing as a result of this particular activity? Are there other members of the same population otherwise engaged? Third, what do those who take part think and feel about their actions? Fourth, how is their behaviour expressly related to their reasons for taking part? Finally, are there any patterns of behaviour involved of which the participants are partially or completely unaware but which nevertheless can be seen by an outside observer as essential to the continuation of the activity?

A scheme of this kind has been applied in the discussion above and in *Village on the Border*. Thus the participants in a football committee meeting are drawn from among the men. Not all the men can be involved and there is a class dimension imposed by the manual nature of the committee's tasks. Men become involved partly out of an interest in football, but also because of relationships of kin and friendship engendered in other situations. Second, they choose football at a particular time as against other activities which have existed or will exist again. Third, they aim to promote by their meeting the holding of football matches. They become emotionally committed to this aim and to the aim of keeping the football club going as an end in itself. Fourth, the different motivations, leading to the contradiction between fun for local lads, and football to win and gain prestige for club and village, lead also to different and mutually inconsistent actions. Finally, their actions are a resultant of both their expressed aims, and consequences flowing from their social positions, as men and as workers in a steadily declining village economy.

This is not, of course, an analysis: it is an indication of the

147

social areas from which relevant material is collected. No picture of the role of football in national life or of sport in the world 'emerges' from it, but it does open up a prospect for the study of the relations between the small scale and the large scale. In any local activity, such as Christmas or football, which can be observed within a community in Britain, part of the observed behaviour may be regarded as *sui generis* and part as being a more or less distorted performance of national norms and mores. The nature of this distortion repays study to illuminate what Goffman has, in a slightly different context, called the rules of transformation (Goffman, 1961, p. 29).

VIII

CONCLUSION: DRAMA AND CONTINUUM
SYNTHESIZED

In conclusion, the problem of synthesis in British community studies is the problem of making micro-sociology (Firth, 1944) relevant to macro-sociology. The two major approaches I have discussed are complementary. The continuum I set up represents an attempt to illuminate the differences between those very rural and less rural areas of Britain which happen to have been studied. This is intrinsically interesting but may also throw light on what British society in general is like and on the processes of social change. I have in effect set up two models and placed the communities I am concerned with in what I consider to be the correct positions between the two. But models are not theories, and social anthropologists are not historians. Wright Mills succinctly puts the former point and George Homans the latter.

Mills wrote:

'A model is a more or less systematic inventory of the elements to which we must pay attention if we are to understand something. It is not true or false; it is useful and adequate to varying degrees. A theory, in contrast, is a statement which can be proved true or false, about the causal weight and the relations of the elements of a model.' (1962, p. 36).

Homans writes:

'. . . there are now two main methods of studying social behaviour, one specialising, upon the whole, on types of institution, concerned with time series, and mainly non-comparative; another specialising on the contemporary, concerned with the interrelations of institutions and often comparative in its emphasis. The former is history, the latter sociology' (Homans, 1953, p. 33; 1962, p. 146).

The methods of studying modern Britain I have put forward seem to me to make up an orthodox and useful social anthropological approach. They are supplementary to the historical approach and to the more sociologically orthodox macrosociological approach of choosing measurable indices (Moser & Scott, 1962; Marsh, 1958; Carr-Saunders, Jones & Moser, 1958). The last method is equivalent to the 'Black Box' approach of the engineer who 'gets a lot of information about a transmission unit simply by comparing the signals that go in with the signals that come out. He often calls the unknown unit a Black Box, and undertakes to determine its performance, by measurements at its input and output terminals without looking inside' (Grey Walter, 1961, p. 142). By using models and dramatic incident we are attempting to see what goes on inside the Black Boxes. Not only our models may be inadequate; and this may partly be because we do not have enough boxes to look into.

However large scale the society we wish to study and however massive the residential unit, there is always social interaction in small face-to-face groups (cp. Laslett, 1956). A limited social area is in no way synonymous with a limited geographical area. Crisis and ceremonial (in the broadest sense) give us the opportunity to observe, in microcosm and dynamically, the often slow-moving and diffuse processes of complex industrial society.

By a familiar paradox, only the most intensive studies of very limited areas of social life will make the most extensive comparative work possible.

Ronald Frankenberg

ACKNOWLEDGEMENTS

Thanks are due to those concerned for permission to quote passages from the following works: Cohen & West Limited in respect of *Structure and Function in Primitive Society* by A. R. Radcliffe-Brown; Dr Maurice Freedman and the Editor of the *British Journal of Sociology* in respect of 'A Chinese Phase in Social Anthropology'.

REFERENCES

ARENSBERG, C. M. 1937. *The Irish Countryman*. New York: Macmillan (reprinted Gloucester, Mass.: Peter Smith, 1959).
— 1961. The Community as Object and as Sample. *American Anthropologist* **63**: 241-264.
ARENSBERG, C. M. & SOLON, T. KIMBALL. 1948. *Family and Community in Ireland*. Cambridge, Mass.: Harvard University Press.
BARNES, J. A. 1954. Class and Committees in a Norwegian Island Parish. *Human Relations* **7**: 39-58.
— 1958. Social Anthropology in Theory and Practice: An inaugural Lecture. *Arts*, the proceedings of the Sydney University Arts Association **1**: 47-67.
BELL, D. A. 1962. *Intelligent Machines*. London: Pitman.
BIRCH, A. H. 1959. *Small-Town Politics*. Oxford: Oxford University Press.
BOTT, ELIZABETH. 1957. *Family and Social Network*. London: Tavistock.
BOTTOMORE, T. B. 1954. Social Stratification in Voluntary Organisation. In David Glass (ed.), *Social Mobility in Britain*. London: Routledge & Kegan Paul.
— 1962. *Sociology: A Guide to Problems and Literature*. London: Allen & Unwin.
BRADNEY, P. 1957a. The Joking Relationship in Industry. *Human Relations* **10**: 179-187.
— 1957b. Quasi-Familial Relationships in Industry. *Human Relations* **10**: 271-278.
CARR-SAUNDERS, A. M., JONES, J. C. & MOSER, C. A. 1958. *A Survey of Social Conditions in England and Wales as illustrated by Statistics*. Oxford: Clarendon Press.
CHERRY, C. 1961. *On Human Communication*. New York: Science Editions (first published 1957).
COLLISON, P. 1963. *The Cutteslowe Walls*. London: Faber & Faber.

DENNIS, N. 1958. The Popularity of the Neighbourhood Community Idea. *Sociological Review* n.s. **6**: 191-206.

—— 1961. Changes in Function and Leadership Renewal. *Sociological Review* n.s. **9**: 55-84.

DENNIS, N., HENRIQUES, FERNANDO, & SLAUGHTER, C. 1957. *Coal is Our Life*. London: Eyre & Spottiswoode.

DEVONS, E. 1950. *Planning in Practice*. Cambridge: Cambridge University Press.

DURANT, RUTH. 1939. *Watling: A Social Survey.* London: P. S. King.

EISENSTADT, S. N. 1961. Anthropological Studies of Complex Societies. *Current Anthropology* **2**: 201-222.

EMMETT, I. 1964. *A North Wales Parish*. London: Routledge & Kegan Paul.

EVANS-PRITCHARD, E. E. 1940. *The Nuer*. Oxford: Clarendon Press.

—— 1949. *The Sanusi of Cyrenaica*. Oxford: Clarendon Press.

FIRTH, RAYMOND. 1944. The Future of Social Anthropology. *Man* article no. 8.

—— 1951. *Elements of Social Organisation*. London: Watts.

FRANKENBERG, R. 1957. *Village on the Border*. London: Cohen & West.

—— 1963. The handling of conflict in decision-making groups: the village and the Nation. British Association Paper (Mimeographed) Aberdeen.

—— 1966. *British Communities*. Harmondsworth: Penguin Books.

FREEDMAN, M. 1963. A Chinese Phase in Social Anthropology. *British Journal of Sociology* **14**: 1-19.

GERTH, H. & LANDAU, SAUL. 1959. The Relevance of History to the Sociological Ethos. In Maurice Stein & Arthur Vidich (eds.), *Sociology on Trial*. Englewood Cliffs, N.J.: Prentice-Hall, 1963.

GIRLING, F. K. 1957. Joking Relationships in a Scottish Town. *Man* article no. 120.

GLASS, D. V. (ed.). 1954. *Social Mobility in Britain*. London: Routledge & Kegan Paul.

GLASS, RUTH. 1955. Urban Sociology. *Current Sociology* **4** Paris: UNESCO.

GLASS, R. (ed.). 1964. *London: Aspects of Change*. London: MacGibbon & Kee.

GLASS, RUTH & FRENKEL, MAUREEN. 1946. How they Live at Bethnal Green. In *Britain between East and West*. London: Contact Books.

GLUCKMAN, M. 1940, 1942. *Analysis of a Social Situation in Modern Zululand*. Reprinted as Rhodes-Livingstone paper No. 28. Manchester, 1958.

Ronald Frankenberg

GLUCKMAN, M. 1954. *Rituals of Rebellion in South East Africa* (The Frazer Lecture, 1952). Manchester: Manchester University Press.

— 1955a. *Custom and Conflict in Africa*. Oxford: Blackwell.

— 1955b. *The Judicial Process among the Barotse of Northern Rhodesia*. Manchester: Manchester University Press, for Rhodes-Livingstone Institute.

— 1961. Ethnographic Data in British Social Anthropology. *Sociological Review* n.s. 9: 5-17 (read at International Sociological Congress, Stresa, 1959).

GOFFMAN, ERVING. 1959. *The Presentation of Self in Everyday Life*. New York: Doubleday (first published Edinburgh 1956).

— 1961. *Encounters*. Indiana: Bobbs Merrill.

HARRIS, ROSEMARY. 1961. The Selection of Leaders in Ballybeg, Northern Ireland. *Sociological Review* n.s. 9: 137-149.

HARRISSON, TOM. 1961. *Britain Revisited*. London: Gollancz.

HOMANS, G. C. 1953. The Rural Sociology of Mediaeval England. *Past and Present* 4: 32-43.

— 1962. *Sentiments and Activities*. London: Routledge & Kegan Paul.

JENNINGS, H. 1962. *Societies in the Making*. London: Routledge & Kegan Paul.

JENNINGS, H. & MADGE, CHARLES. 1937. *May the Twelfth*. London: Faber & Faber.

LITTLEJOHN, J. 1964. *Westrigg*. London: Routledge & Kegan Paul.

LOUDON, J. 1961. Kinship and Crisis in South Wales. *British Journal of Sociology* 12: 333-349.

MADGE, CHARLES & HARRISSON, TOM (eds.). 1939. *Britain*. London: Penguin Books.

MALINOWSKI, B. 1938. A Nation-wide Intelligence Service. In *First Year's Work by Mass Observation*. London: Lindsay Drummond.

MARRIS, P. 1958. *Widows and their Families*. London: Routledge & Kegan Paul.

MARSH, D. C. 1958. *The Changing Social Structure of England and Wales*. London: Routledge & Kegan Paul.

MARSHALL, T. H. 1950. *Citizenship and Social Class*. Cambridge: Cambridge University Press.

MERTON, R. K. 1957a. *Social Theory & Social Structure*. 2nd Edition. Glencoe, Ill.: Free Press.

— 1957b. The Role-Set: Problems in Sociological Theory. *British Journal of Sociology* 8: 106-120.

MILLS, C. WRIGHT. 1959. *The Sociological Imagination*. New York: Oxford University Press.

—— 1962. *The Marxists*. Harmondsworth: Penguin; New York: Dell.

MITCHELL, J. CLYDE. 1956. *The Kalela Dance*. Rhodes-Livingstone Paper No. 27. Manchester: Manchester University Press.

MOSER, C. A. & SCOTT, WOLF. 1961. *British Towns*. Edinburgh: Oliver & Boyd.

NADEL, S. F. 1951. *The Foundations of Social Anthropology*. London: Cohen & West.

—— 1957. *The Theory of Social Structure*. London: Cohen & West.

PARKINSON, C. NORTHCOTE. 1960. Article in *The Director*, June, London.

PLOWMAN, D. E. G., MINCHINTON, W. E. & STACEY, MARGARET. 1962. Local Social Status in England and Wales. *Sociological Review* n.s. **10**: 161-202.

PONS, VALDO. 1961. Two small groups in Avenue 21. In Aidan Southall (ed.), *Social Change in Modern Africa*. London: Oxford University Press, for International African Institute.

RADCLIFFE-BROWN, A. R. 1952. *Structure and Function in Primitive Society*. London: Cohen & West.

REES, A. D. 1951. *Life in a Welsh Countryside*. Cardiff: University of Wales Press.

ROBB, J. H. 1954. *Working-Class Anti-Semite*. London: Tavistock Publications.

SAMPSON, A. 1962. *The Anatomy of Britain*. London: Hodder.

SNOW, C. P. 1961. *Science and Government*. London: Oxford University Press.

—— 1962. *A Postscript to Science and Government*. London: Oxford University Press.

SOUTHALL, AIDAN. 1959. An Operational Theory of Role. *Human Relations* **12**: 17-34.

SPENCER, J. 1964. *Stress and Release in an Urban Estate*. London: Tavistock Publications.

STACEY, MARGARET. 1960. *Tradition and Change*. Oxford: Oxford University Press.

STEIN, MAURICE R. 1960. *The Eclipse of Community*. Princeton, N.J.: Princeton University Press.

TOWNSEND, P. 1957. *The Family Life of Old People*. London: Routledge & Kegan Paul.

TURNER, V. W. 1957. *Schism and Continuity in an African Society*. Manchester: Manchester University Press.

VALLEE, F. G. 1955. Burial and Mourning Customs in a Hebridean Community. *Journal of the Royal Anthropological Institute* **85**: 119-130.

WALTER, W. GREY. 1961. *The Living Brain*. Harmondsworth: Penguin Books.

WATSON, W. 1960. The Managerial Spiralist. *The Twentieth Century*, London.

—— 1964. Social Mobility and Social Class in Industrial Communities. In E. Devons & M. Gluckman (eds.), *Closed Systems and Open Minds*. Edinburgh: Oliver & Boyd. (Read as ASA paper 1957.)

WILLIAMS, W. M. 1956. *The Sociology of an English Village*. London: Routledge & Kegan Paul.

—— 1963. *A West Country Village: Ashworthy*. London: Routledge & Kegan Paul.

WILLMOTT, P. 1963. *The Evolution of a Community*. London: Routledge & Kegan Paul.

WILLMOTT, P. & YOUNG, MICHAEL. 1960. *Family and Class in a London Suburb*. London: Routledge & Kegan Paul.

WILSON, R. 1963. *Difficult Housing Estates*. Pamphlet No. 5. London: Tavistock Publications.

YOUNG, MICHAEL & WILLMOTT, PETER. 1957. *Family and Kinship in East London*. London: Routledge & Kegan Paul.

NOTES ON CONTRIBUTORS

BENEDICT, BURTON. Born 1923. U.S.A.; educated at Harvard University, A.B.; London, Ph.D.

Senior Research Fellow, Institute of Islamic Studies, McGill University, 1954-5; Assistant Lecturer in Anthropology, London School of Economics, 1958; Lecturer, 1961; Senior Lecturer, 1964.

Author of *Indians in a Plural Society*, 1961.

EGGAN, FRED. Born 1906, Seattle, Washington; studied at The University of Chicago, B.A., M.A., Ph.D.

Harold H. Swift Distinguished Service Professor of Anthropology and Director, Philippine Studies Program, University of Chicago.

Author of *Social Organization of the Western Pueblos*, 1950; 'Social Anthropology and the Method of Controlled Comparison' (*American Anthropologist*, Vol. 56, 1954); 'Social Anthropology: Methods and Results' (in *Social Anthropology of North American Tribes*, 1955);

Editor of *Social Anthropology of North American Tribes*, 1937, Enlarged Edition, 1955.

FRANKENBERG, RONALD. Born 1929, London. Studied at Gonville and Caius College, Cambridge, B.A.; and Manchester University, M.A.(Econ.), Ph.D.; Research Assistant, University College, Cardiff, 1954-6; Education Officer in Trade Union 1957-60; since 1960 Lecturer in Sociology at Manchester University.

Author of *Village on the Border*, 1957; *British Communities* (in press).

GLUCKMAN, MAX. Born 1911, South Africa; studied at The University of Witwatersrand, B.A.; Oxford, D.Phil.

Anthropologist, Rhodes-Livingstone Institute, 1939-42; Director, 1942-7; Lecturer in Social Anthropology, Oxford, 1947-9; Professor of Social Anthropology, Manchester, 1949.

Author of *The Judicial Process among the Barotse of N. Rhodesia*, 1954; *Custom and Conflict in Africa*, 1955; *Order and Rebellion in Tribal Africa*, 1963; *Politics, Law and Ritual in Tribal Societies*, 1965; *The Ideas in Barotse Jurisprudence*, 1965. Editor of *Seven Tribes of British Central Africa*, 1951; *Closed Systems and Open Minds*, 1964.

Notes on Contributors

LOUDON, JOSEPH BUIST. Born 1921, Wales; educated at Oxford University, B.A. (Natural Science), M.A., B.M., B.Ch.; London University (London School of Economics), Diploma in Anthropology.

Medical appointments, 1946-56; Assistant Lecturer in Social Anthropology, London School of Economics, 1956-7; Social Anthropologist, Social Psychiatry Research Unit, Medical Research Council, 1957-64; Lecturer in Social Anthropology, University College, Swansea, 1964.

MAYER, ADRIAN C. Born 1922, England. Studied at St. John's College, Annapolis, Md., U.S.A., B.A.; London, Ph.D.

Scholar, Australian National University, 1950; Research Fellow, 1953; Lecturer, School of Oriental & African Studies, University of London, 1956; Reader in Indian Anthropology, 1962.

Author of *Land and Society in Malabar*, 1952; *Caste and Kinship in Central India*, 1960; *Peasants in the Pacific*, 1961; *Indians in Fiji*, 1963.

MITCHELL, JAMES CLYDE. Born 1918, South Africa; studied at Natal University College B.A. (Soc. Sc.) and the University of South Africa, B.A. (Hons.) Sociology; Oxford, D.Phil.

Appointments at Rhodes-Livingstone Research Institute: Assistant Anthropologist, 1945; Senior Sociologist, 1950; Director, 1952-5. Simon Research Fellow, Manchester University, 1953; Professor of African Studies, University College of Rhodesia and Nyasaland, 1955-65; Professor of Urban Sociology, Manchester University, 1966.

Author of *The Yao Village*, 1956; *The Kalela Dance*, 1956.

WOLF, ERIC ROBERT. Born 1923, Austria; studied at Queens College, New York, B.A.; Columbia University, Ph.D.

Assistant Professor, University of Illinois, 1952-5; University of Virginia, 1955-8; Yale University, 1958-9; Associate Professor, University of Chicago, 1959-61; Professor, University of Michigan since 1961. Fieldwork in Puerto Rico, 1948-9; Mexico, 1951-2, 1954, 1956; Italian Alps, 1960-1.

Author of *Sons of the Shaking Earth*, 1959; *Anthropology*, 1964.